Dear Kim
You have & always will
be very special to us. Keep close
to Jesus & He'll direct your steps. Prov. 3:5,6
We love you very much!
Pen & Joanne

MOMENTS
WITH
MAJESTY

ip His Majesty

Jack Hayford

MOMENTS WITH MAJESTY

MULTNOMAH

Portland, Oregon

glory, honor, and

Cover design and calligraphy by Bill McConaughy and Dave Anderson

Edited by Larry R. Libby

MOMENTS WITH MAJESTY
© 1990 by Jack Hayford
Published by Multnomah Press
Portland, Oregon 97266

Multnomah Press is a ministry of Multnomah School of the Bible, 8435 N.E. Glisan Street, Portland, Oregon 97220

Printed in the United States

Library of Congress Cataloging-in-Publication Data

Hayford, Jack W.
    Moments with majesty / Jack Hayford.
       p.   cm.
    ISBN 0-88070-365-2
    1. Meditations.   I. Title.
    BV4832.2.H35345   1990
    242'.2—dc20   90-34174
                                                          CIP

90 91 92 93 94 95 96 97 98 99   10 9 8 7 6 5 4 3 2 1

To the Father
        who gave us Son,
To the Son,
        who gave us life, and
To the Holy Spirit,
        who gave me the song

if

kingdom authority —

flow from His

JANUARY

Expectation

FEBRUARY

Comfort

MARCH

Remembrance

APRIL

Growth

MAY

Power

JUNE

Triumph

raise, So exalt,

JULY

Praise

AUGUST

Prayer

lift up on high

SEPTEMBER

Contemplation

OCTOBER

Faith

GRATITUDE

This book is a special delight, fulfilling a lifetime dream to have a "book of thoughts," which may feed the soul, refresh the spirit, and renew the mind of the Father's children.

It is the result of the vision of a marvelous team of people at Multnomah: Brenda Jose, who conceived the idea; Larry Libby, whose masterful editing arranged the manuscript; and John Van Diest, whose trust and brotherly kindness opened the door for its publication.

But beyond anyone else who made this possible is my beloved and respected daughter, Rebecca Bauer. It was Becki who culled through a scrambled pile of past year's church bulletins and gleaned the material to fashion the book. The work she undertook and the outstanding job she did is a major accomplishment on any terms—but all the more so for a busy pastor's wife and the mother of three school-age children.

Her sensitivity, discernment, and precise and efficient attention to multitudinous details are a testimony to her skills, her commitment, and her spiritual and practical wisdom. But her doing so with such dedication is also a testimony of her love for her dad and her belief in the worth of his work. Thank you, Becki. For that I'm *more* than grateful. I'm humbled.

God bless each of you who allow me to serve Him and His larger Flock—His Body, the Church.

INTRODUCTION

The atmosphere was impregnated with an ennobling air of royalty! It was impossible to be there and not to feel a sense of destiny in the rooms of the giant castle.

Those are my own words, describing my visit to Churchill's boyhood home at Blenheim Palace, in Oxfordshire, England. It was this setting which ignited thoughts resulting in the composition of the song "Majesty." What began as a look at history and the way one man was raised to influence it so dramatically, grew into this thought: Environment ennobles, creating a sense of personal significance.

I was thinking of how Churchill's early home life in such a regal setting would have contributed to his own perspective on himself. Then my thought leaped to the fact that *we* are daily invited to walk and talk with royalty. Suddenly I was stirred. *Majesty! HIS majesty, whom I worship, not only welcomes my fellowship, but wants to infuse my life with purpose and power as I bow in His presence!*

It was an added degree of insight, extending a discovery made only a few years before: God summons us to His throne for *our* sake, not for His.

That was new to me. I had always presumed—indeed, been taught—that worship was due the Almighty, that we ought to render it dutifully as an offering to His glory.

Of course that's true, and right to do.

But an addendum to this obvious truth was the discovery that God calls us to spend moments in His presence because of *our* need and benefit, not His.

His Majesty, Jesus Christ our Lord, calls us to abide in Him, walk with Him, wait on Him, think with Him, revel in joyous song in His presence, and bow in heartfelt adoration at His feet. The objective: to transform us, renew us, and fulfill us.

Moments with Majesty —

. . . times my soul spends in quietness *beside* Him, that I
might gain confidence *from* Him;

. . . seasons when my heart is humbled *before* Him, that I
might be lifted *by* Him.

The essence of those moments distills in two words: *worship* and *worth*. We worship Him because He is completely worthy; He enables us, bringing worth to our lives.

Catch the vision . . . a subject of a king, kneeling in allegiance before his enthroned master. The monarch rises, his jeweled scepter in one hand, his mighty sword in the other. Laying the sword on each of his subject's bowing shoulders, he declares his will to raise this citizen of his kingdom into nobility. Knighted! Raised to royal recognition by the will of the king!

So Jesus Christ invites us to be with Him. He summons us to enter His presence, to open our hearts to the insights of His Word, to sing our soul's exaltation of His glories, and to bow before Him, receiving His fresh commissioning.

These pages are offered to assist you toward such encounters with His Majesty—Jesus Christ, King of the Universe.

They were written over nearly two decades, selected from week to week sojourns of thought I recorded for the encouragement of my congregation. But as the years have gone by, the letters from people who have read these "Left-Hand Pages" (so called, for that is where they first appeared in our weekly bulletin) have indicated a potential far beyond local application. I trust you'll find this equally true.

As you read, I hope most of all you will be *lifted*—

. . . lifted to new heights of joy in Jesus,

. . . lifted to new perspective on your own potential in
Him,

. . . lifted to new dimensions of love in knowing Him, and

. . . lifted to a new sense of worth and dignity in being His!

Here's a book which will bring refreshing and renewal. It was written by a plain shepherd for his pasturing sheep. But the goal is for ordinary citizens of God's Kingdom to rise to new heights as His extraordinary ones—the ones whom divine Royalty has honored and raised to richer purpose and higher destiny.

JANUARY

Expectation

who died now

Lord,
You cause my heart to laugh
*   and make my mouth to sing.*
For the joy of Your way
*   increases ev'ry day*
And I find my hands
*   are reaching out in love.*

glorified, Kin

Expectancy

And my speech and my preaching were not with persuasive words of human wisdom, but in demonstration of the Spirit and of power (1 Corinthians 2:4).

True New Testament ministry requires *results*.

It is not theory, it is action. Paul's words exhort me . . . and you.

To those who teach, Paul says, "Don't deceive yourself by thinking you're through when you've preached or taught. Press for follow-through! Expect life change!"

To those who listen, the message says, "Don't deceive yourself by thinking it is enough to be taught or to hear. The hearing of faith responds. Expect God's hand at work—in you and through you."

I'm feeling very expectant as I write these words. The Holy Spirit is pressing His people—all of us—to move together toward a new season of manifest miracles glorifying Jesus in our midst.

It won't come without conflict. It won't happen without spiritual warfare. We must possess the land in *Jesus' name.*

Then Jesus came and spoke to them, saying, "All authority has been given to Me in heaven and on earth. . . . Go into all the world . . . And these signs will follow those who believe: In My name . . ." (Matthew 28:18; Mark 16:15, 17).

Let the name of Jesus begin to stir new confidence in your life today. He has granted that instrument—His own name—as the signature, the badge of authority, the security, the guarantee of every promise offered us in the Word. And in that name, we are to expect *results.* In our life. In our family. In our neighborhood. In our church. In our world.

Yes, there is a waiting of faith, a patience of hope, and a fellowship of those who learn to abide in the assurance of God's goodness—even when answers are not immediately forthcoming. But there are also times to expect action.

Let me urge you to be open to such a time for you. Today. Now.

Expect with me. Boldly believe!

Hearing The Invisible

OPTASIA: Meno! Greetings. Come in—sit down. The announcement of your return and our appointment has just preceded you. I'm expectant about our conversation—and to know of the progress on your assignment.

MENO: Thank you, Optasia. The Father's summons directed I return from earth for a brief season, particularly to counsel with you regarding the project.

OPTASIA: Let's see, this concerns the people who call themselves "The Church On The Way," correct? As I recall, they have become a people who please the Father and have permitted us to work with them.

MENO: That is true, but my coming has to do with essential steps they must be taking soon—or that report will become historical rather than current. True, they have received our angelic aid to labor with them in spiritual ministry and spiritual warfare. Now, it appears we must decide how we can help alert them.

OPTASIA: Alert them to the Laodicean Syndrome, you mean? Yes . . . that seems to be a constant threat to the fruitfulness of this mortal breed. You would think the Son's warning to them in the Revelation would be adequate, but they fall prey to it so often.

MENO: Somehow the accomplishment of certain works and the walking in a beginning of wisdom tends to lull redeemed humans toward spiritual drowsiness. What is the Father's directive at this point?

OPTASIA: He has done nothing more at this point than to direct our counseling together. They are your assignment, and, as your own name indicates, the Father has committed Himself to abide with that people in a distinct way. As your fellow laborer, I have been told to join you in seeking to advance His will.

MENO: Then that accounts for my privilege in working with you in particular, Optasia. For your gift is the awakening and enlargement of vision . . . as they on earth call it, "seeing the invisible." My knowledge of this people would recommend our first line of strategy be an effort in our realm which will goad them in their realm.

OPTASIA: Most of them, I would guess from the report, are either forgetful or ignorant of the fact that their worship, their prayer, their unbound seasons of intercession and supplication, that these—well, has the pastor taught them concerning the fact that their world is invaded with power when they do these things?

MENO: Yes, he has. But some of the more mature ones fall into neglect and sterile habit, and often their new ones—they are a growing flock, with many babes in spiritual understanding—are not as careful to hear the deep truths they should be growing on. However, Optasia, I feel that your gift for restoring and revealing sight is what we need to bring to bear upon their situation.

OPTASIA: Fine. I believe the Father's mind on the matter is coming to us, and we know we have the Third One's blessing on our effort, since it is the First's directive that we take this assignment together. . . .

And like earphones pulled from a stereo, the invisible realm tunes out. I sit back, listening to the buzz of voices outside my door, a passing car outside, and a jangling telephone. My supposedly "real" world crowds in.

But before I set aside my musings, I breathe a quick prayer. *Lord, grant me eyes to see the real battles, the real issues, the real dangers, the real opportunities that intersect my path a thousand times a day. Wake me from a sleepy, careless state of mind. Protect me from the hypnotic hum of activities that make the eyes of my heart grow heavy. I ask it for me . . . that I might warn those I love.*

God's Give-Away Program

Our American culture is unique to most parts of the world in many ways, not the least of which is our bombastic, super-galaxy-of-gifts, television giveaway programs.

Unto Jesus he

As commercial and Madison-Avenue-packaged as they are, I must confess that in at least a couple of respects this cultural trait mirrors something of God's methods.

I see two parallels: (1) The recipient receives something free, and (2) the giver distributes from the abundance of his resources.

Theologically, we would call the first "grace," and the second "omnipotence." What God gives us is completely unearned, and the way He gives is from the abounding provision of the Almighty, All-Sufficient One.

From the moment of my entry into the saving life Jesus has given me through the Cross, all the way through my lifetime of learning to walk in His love and power . . . it's all grace. He gives it. Nothing is earned. Nothing is actuated by my strength or power. As the hymnwriter put it, "He giveth, and giveth, and giveth again."

And, of course, the second feature of this tandem-truth is the resource from which He gives. It's boundless, measureless, unlimited, unending, abundant, almighty, and eternal.

Be comforted and emboldened in your faith, friend. God has gifts for you and in quantities you never dreamed. These gifts are infinitely more valuable than the tinsel and materialistic toys pursued so desperately by the world. He has gifts of peace, strength, joy, fulfillment, and a sense of significance in life that will draw you out of bed each morning like a magnet.

He's looking for people who will come in simple dependence upon His grace, and rest in simple faith upon His greatness.

At this very moment, He's looking at you.

glory, honor and

The Day Will Come

I was moved some time ago by the report that during the visit of Pope John Paul II to Japan, he visited an ailing eighty-three-year-old Polish friar who has spent more than fifty years helping the poor and destitute of Japan. Zeno Zebrowski, frail from a heart ailment and confined to a wheelchair, broke into tears as his Polish compatriot greeted him—kissing Zebrowski's cheek and grasping the aged priest's hand in prayer.

Brother Zeno had been laboring in Japan in the service of the Lord Jesus for more than fifty years, having arrived there in 1930. He survived the atomic bomb attack on Nagasaki which climaxed World War II, and in the confusing period which followed was instrumental in organizing the bombed-out poor into communities developed to assist in reconstruction.

The Pope, formerly Cardinal Wojtyla and archbishop of Krakow, Poland, said, "Zeno, I wanted very much to meet you. I am very grateful for the great work you have done here." This greeting followed the pontiff's entry into the room with the words, *"The Pope from Poland has come."*

Zeno wept as he received his visitor.

My eyes filled also when I read this report. My heart leaped to think of the meaning of this visit to the wearied servant whose life has been given in the service of the Lord.

Yet even as I read of this meeting, I envisioned a similar day . . . a grander day.

I thought of people like you and me who are sometimes weary—feeling alone, unrewarded. Men and women who, in spite of hardship and loneliness, continue at their post without complaint, faithful in the service of King Jesus.

And I thought, the day will come when through the doorway of the heavenlies this One will come again. He will make His announcement: "The Lord from Glory has come!" And He will take our hands, and greet us with a holy kiss—count on it, Church—and say, "Well done, good and faithful servant. Enter into the joy of your Lord. You have been faithful over few things, I will make you ruler over many things."

Lift up your eyes! And keep your hand fixed to the plow of constant service. Look! His return is near—even at the door!

Rivers of Pentecost

In describing the Holy Spirit's coming, Jesus specifically said, "Rivers of living water shall flow from the inner being of all those who believe me" (John 7:37-38, paraphrase). On Pentecost, what Joel had prophesied, Peter preached: "God has poured out His Spirit—a stream of restoring, healing power is released to mankind!"(Joel 2, Acts 2, paraphrase).

Just recently I knelt in prayer, moved to ask God, concerning these "rivers of Pentecost":

Lord, flow forth fresh watercourses of Holy Spirit fullness and power in my life.

Let the flow bear me forward. I don't want to become a stagnant pool of former blessing, but a rising river of fresh inspiration.

Let the rivers run deep. I don't want to be shallow in any part of my life. Let the sandbars of carnal obstruction in my nature be furrowed out by the force of the stream.

Let me learn to flow together with other believers, as streams become tributaries to a larger river. Let any smallness become lost in my surrender to Your Spirit's blending me with all those who love You in truth. Let me move with them in the unity of Jesus' life and love.

Let me be a channel.

In a world where the blind and the bound seek "spirit-channels" to touch the realm of the supernatural and thereby only become more confused, let me be a pure channel of Holy Spirit life and truth. Let me bring the wholeness of who You really are, in Jesus' name.

Come, Holy Spirit . . . as rivers of living water.

He Shall Be Great... Therefore!

The echo of the angelic announcement concerning Jesus rings in our ears: "He shall be GREAT and shall be called the Son of the Highest!"

By virtue of the inescapable GREATNESS of our Savior, a resounding "therefore" rises from my lips today.

We have a GREAT SAVIOR . . .

. . . *Therefore* we are possessors of a great salvation, which encompasses every dimension of human need and deserves to be broadcast to every circle where people hurt.

. . . *Therefore* we are encouraged to expect great victories, knowing that great battles are necessary for conquest, but confident because He is leading us.

These two "therefores" provide a focus I ask you to share with me today and into this whole year.

The first has to do with our *faith* as believers—moving forward in prayer, intercession, and giving, because the possessing of possibilities requires it.

The second has to do with our *reach* as believers—extending ourselves to touch others, because He has so mightily touched us with His grace and goodness.

LET THIS BE A YEAR OF GROWTH AND HARVEST!

— Growing in our walk with Jesus—staying close to Him.

— Growing in the Word of God—deepening in understanding.

— Growing in faith, prayer, and boldness in giving.

— Growing in loving, serving, and helping those we can.

— Reaching by every means and media to touch our city or town.

— Touching the lost in the confidence His power will save.

— Caring for people who long for someone who will.

— Showing the love of Jesus in ways which gain us the right to be heard, so we can tell of His salvation.

Walk with me and think with me over this thought: There is nothing too great for us to expect since we have so great a Savior and Lord.

Starting Over

I hear a loud, clear call of the Spirit these days: "Repent and do the first works" (Revelation 2:5).

It resounds from the heart of Jesus and summons from the written Word of God. It is a herald to us for these beginning weeks of a new year.

We are standing on holy ground. By any measure or estimate, we have come through a cycle of years. I can put my finger on a number of such cycles:

. . . The years since Anna and I received our call to ministry.

. . . The years since we began our service here at The Church On The Way.

. . . The years since our congregation received a special intercessory assignment from the Lord.

You supply your own numbers and milestones. How many years since you surrendered to Jesus as Lord of your life . . . since you stood and repeated vows before the Lord with the one who would become your life partner . . . since His Spirit led you into the church where you find fellowship . . . since you turned your back on some besetting sin . . . since you submitted to the Spirit's call for a special area of service?

That cycle of years is, I am convinced by the Lord, intended to bring us to a place of starting over. Please note that I said *starting over*. I did not say *beginning again*.

Is there a difference? Oh, yes.

To *start over* is to return to your roots and nourish them. It is to assure yourself that you remember what it is that makes you tick.

For senators and congressional representatives, it's getting back to their home states and districts; walking the streets, neighborhoods, boroughs, parishes, and precincts. It's sipping coffee with citizens in the diners and lunch-rooms. It's getting behind the mike on local radio call-in programs, and holding town meetings.

For professional athletes, it's participating in off-season camps and clinics and drills that reemphasize the fundamentals of the game.

For Monopoly buffs, it's returning to "GO" and, best of all, "collecting $200!"

Starting over doesn't involve loss, but it does require humility. And that has an assured reward.

Beginning again, on the other hand, is what you do when a tornado destroys the farm. When a storm washes away the bridge. When an earthquake rips the house off its foundation. When moral failure poisons the purity of trust in a relationship.

The Lord, who calls us to return to those things which His Word teaches and which release the power of His presence among us, is not making a statement about anything being so lost, ruined, or wrecked that there is nothing of spiritual capital with which to start afresh.

But He is saying that our assignment is to become as children all over again. To kneel again at the altar of our first commitment. To return to our first love. To perform our first works.

So renewed, we will be mightily released unto His highest purpose and praise.

On Writing Your Book

Have you heard about the book we're writing?

I don't mean the book projects I've tackled with various Christian publishers. I mean the one *we* are writing. You. Me. Us. We. Those of us who own Jesus as Savior and Lord.

A book opens before us today. This month. This new year. It is a book with blank pages.

The Lord has said He will print and publish it. He will accomplish it by *His power*. He is waiting for us to write . . . to reach forth our hand, to inscribe by faith, to respond to His invitation to see a new thing brought forth.

A whole assortment of Bible references rush to mind on writing books of this kind:

• John 21:25 ends with the words, "I suppose that even the world itself could not contain the books that would be written." John was talking about all that Jesus does by His miracle power.

• The Book of Acts begins by asserting its contents are the continuing record of Jesus' doings. Significantly, its twenty-eighth chapter has no "amen" concluding it. The Acts of the Holy Spirit go on and on. Who will write them? Will you?

• Revelation 20:12-13 shows the unsaved being judged from books that were written by their life-deeds.

• Second Corinthians 3:2,3 indicates clearly that our lives are letters that are being written and declared-indeed to those around us.

• Matthew 25:14-30 reveals how Jesus will settle the

books with us at His return. We will be judged as to how faithful we have been with the life-ministry opportunities He has entrusted to us through the years.

All of this points to one disturbing, challenging fact:

The sovereign God of the universe has committed Himself to write the history of earth. But He has willed to do it through human instruments, and invites you and me to respond with chapters of bold accomplishments done in Jesus' Name.

You probably feel as I do, when such an enormous truth begins to dawn upon you: "What can I do? It's too much for me."

But wait. Remember, the power is HIS. He is the Publisher. He's simply looking for writers; for people who will trust the power of His Holy Spirit to work in the common, ordinary affairs of their daily lives—family, business, relationships, schoolwork, difficulties, ministry opportunities.

It's because these mundane details of life are the decisive, history-making points of life that we teach as we do: Your ministry *is* significant. Wonderfully, frighteningly significant.

God offers to you and me—to all who live—-a blank book of possibilities, and now asks what we are going to write. Let's write with wisdom, and in big letters!

In God's Own Time

Our God is wise beyond all words and great beyond all
worlds.

His pow'r unmeasured by all terms that men can know.

And with a love transcending human understanding or
design,

He rules beyond all time, His perfect will to show.

Chorus:

In God's own time there's more than you can dream;

In His own time there's room for all His will.

So trust in God and say,

"Dear Lord, today I'll wait your perfect ending."

And in His own time, you'll find His time your friend.

His timeless Word extends His promises unto my day,

His sov'reign pow'r is pledged to hold me by His hand.

And while I wait the working of His will He'll keep me
by His side,

Until He brings me unto all that He has planned.

He who created all the seasons in their perfect time;

Who planned the seedtime and the harvest that it
brings;

He who Himself with patience waits the final gathering
of His own

Has taught my heart to wait on Him and gladly sing.

Magnify, come

orify Christ Jesus,

FEBRUARY
Comfort

It's me, Lord,
Just me, Lord;
I long to be free, Lord,
So I come to Thee, Lord,
With my heart in my hands.

Remembering Jade Cove

Anna and I were recently coming back from Carmel, where we celebrated our wedding anniversary. Driving south on Highway 1, that famous roadway that hugs the Pacific Coast, I reminisced as we passed Jade Cove, near Big Sur. That's the place where, years ago, by the grace of God, I "turned the corner." I don't mean a curve on that twisting, perilous highway, but the turn-around at Jade Cove rescued me from something as bad as a car accident.

For several weeks I had been experiencing a horrible accumulation of pressure—mental and emotional. Work had piled up, schedule demands were burning me out. Through a combination of circumstances, I was riding the ragged edge of a nervous breakdown.

Some nights I would dream of being chased—and then crushed—by a massive object relentlessly pursuing and slowly gaining on me as I ran to escape it. Other nights I feared closing my eyes to go to sleep, feeling if I did I would not awaken again—that my heart would stop or my breath cease. I was rational enough to know this wasn't true, but weak enough in my emotionally drained condition that I was unable to break the tormenting thoughts.

Then I discovered the words of the songwriter. Listen . . .

who died now

I will both lie down in peace, and sleep;
For You alone, O LORD, make me dwell in safety
(Psalm 4:8).

And another lyric:

I lay down and slept; I awoke, for the LORD sustained
me (Psalm 3:5).

I can hardly describe the power of those words as they flowed across my weary soul. I grasped them for the reliable, eternal words of truth that they are. They were all the more meaningful to me when I remembered they were written by a very busy man—a man of accomplishment and crushing responsibilities. David was a successful king and a conquering hero, yet a man who needed release from pressures that threatened his sleep.

God's words buoyed my soul for several weeks, sustaining me until that day on Highway 1. I was driving slowly northward, hoping a break in schedule and a change of scene would take the cascading voices off my mind and the rising fear from my heart.

I had stopped at the sign. Jade Cove, it read. I went down near the water's edge to look at the beautiful seascape. To listen to the waves. To feel the sea-spray on my face. To pray.

It was there something happened—better yet, Someone. Because as surely as I knew His Word had sustained me when fear plagued my nights, I knew God's presence had drawn near to deliver my mind. Like fog burning off the coastline, the Son of God simply reached down and lifted the burden I had carried for months.

I share that with you now to urge *you* to receive His Word. "I will both lie down in peace, and sleep; for You alone, O LORD, make me dwell in safety."

Call upon His Holy Spirit to deliver you. I know He will, because He did that for me at a place called Jade

Cove, and He did it through the power of a man named Jesus.

He's there for you. Right now. You don't even have to go to Jade Cove. Because . . .

"Whoever calls on the name of the LORD
shall be saved" (Acts 2:21).

Jesus' words come to my mind today:

If human fathers, who at best are imperfect and fallible, know how to give good gifts to their children, how much more shall the Father give the Holy Spirit to those who ask Him (Matthew 7:11, paraphrase).

In plain words, the Savior was saying that there is no earthly counterpart to either the Father's goodness or His mercy.

Yet so few understand the Father-heart of God.

Jesus said, "[Father,] I have declared to them Your name [Your nature]" (John 17:26). The Gospel-writer writes of Jesus, "The only begotten Son, who is in the bosom of the Father, He has declared Him" (John 1:18). These words notwithstanding, there are still hosts of individuals who have no sense of inner certainty about the manner or the mentality of Father God. So many are dominated by the fearsome image of a stern-countenanced Deity, wielding His scepter in judgment. Yet the Scriptures reply in stark contrast, "Oh, give thanks to the God of heaven! For His mercy endures forever" (Psalm 136:26).

But God isn't Santa Claus either.

Nor is He "the Man Upstairs," nor a syrupy, maudlin, super-grandpa who dodders around heaven in a semi-senile state doling out platitudes about "being nice," or, "anything is all right if you are sincere," or, "love means you never have to say you're sorry."

He is a Father who teaches us, "As the heavens are higher than the earth, so are My ways higher than your ways, and My thoughts than your thoughts" (Isaiah 55:9). In no uncertain terms, He shows us that His viewpoint and wisdom are so many rungs higher than ours, we're foolish unless we *always*

. . . make Him our point of reference for counsel. He has the master plan of our life, and, knowing the end from the beginning, is best prepared to lead us.

. . . trust Him with our destiny. Present trials, suffering, or tragedy may often seem the end—or cause us to wish it were. Yet the Father knows this period isn't the end of a sentence, but a connecting point in the completion of the masterpiece which is His whole story for us.

. . . wait for Him. What strange words. As though He were slow! But the slowness is *our* passage through time—time which He has already transcended. Mysteriously, He is able to both walk with us now, and be stationed at a point down life's road, waiting to welcome us.

In His presence we will be able to look back and say, "Oh. Oh, Father. I see. I see!"

Peace On Earth?

We were both cloaked in heavy coats and scarves as we strode along together, the skies above filled with winking stars etched into the inky backdrop of space.

Christy, our youngest daughter—a junior high school student—was with me as we enjoyed one of our frequent walks—times we both look forward to. She was talking, her remarks initiated by the fact that a friend's house had recently been broken into and robbed.

"Ya know, Dad, it really makes me afra—well, not afraid, but it kinda bothers me when . . . ya know . . . all the stuff that's on the news . . . and when bad things happen, like . . . well, robberies and killing and . . . you know, all that stuff . . . it sorta gets, well, it's so much like . . . I just wish that people would . . . ya know, Dad?"

Then, punctuated by a sudden waving of arms, her voice squeaked higher: "You know what I mean . . . I mean, I wish everything would be peaceful!"

I do know what she meant. It doesn't take the interpretive skill usually necessary to understand a junior high schooler to feel what Christy was talking about. We all get tired of living in a weary world; a world worn by sin and death. A thousand manifestations of those two factors surround us, but the end analysis is always the same: The root is sin in the race and the fruit is death. Sin kills . . . it kills joy, hope, love, trust, peace, and, finally, people.

She continued. "Sometimes I think it would be so-o-o

nice to live somewhere like Chippewa Falls [where her cousins live in Wisconsin]. Ya know, I mean, I like it here in Los Angeles, and all my friends, and our house, and my school, and . . . ya know, Dad."

"I know," I answered.

It was quiet a minute, our footsteps alone breaking the silence. I squeezed her hand reassuringly that I really did know how she felt.

"Chris," I began. "When you visited Amy and David in Chippewa Falls, were there any police cars there?"

She replied that there were, and I asked why she supposed so. She immediately got the point.

"I guess, Dad, because bad things happen everywhere . . . even in Wisconsin."

I went on, trying not to sound too preacherly. "Honey, there's no place in the world you can go to find peacefulness, because there's no place in the world to get away from people who hurt and who hate. Peace isn't something that's around you so much as it is something that is inside you."

We talked a lot more about that, and she evidenced that she really did understand. And was satisfied . . . truly. For peace is knowing (1) you are right with God, (2) you are right in your relationships, and (3) you are living where God wants you to be . . . in His will. The angels' message, "Peace on earth," is not a tease or a taunt where open hearts will let peace work its wonder. And that peace will guard the heart that continues in confident surrender to the Father's will and way (Philippians 4:6,7).

At The Mercy of Love

At your mercy.

The phrase conjures up medieval images, doesn't it? Picture a swordsman, his weapon slapped from his hand, backed up against a wall with his rival's swordpoint against his throat . . . or see a breathless maiden, hands spread outward in pleading helplessness as she spins around and kneels in the center of the forest path along which she has been fleeing her pursuers.

At your mercy.

It suggests uncertain destiny, possible death, or, at best, some manner of enslavement.

It conveys an idea of an unpleasant, although preferable, option—

> . . . an alms, instead of nothing at all;

> . . . a lease-on-life instead of death;

> . . . an opportunity for ransom instead of permanent abduction.

It is something *better* than the worst, but not necessarily good.

The mercy the Scriptures teach, however, is of another kind. It is completely *compassionate*, entirely *benevolent*, and it is totally *paid* for. Best of all, it is an abounding trait of God Himself who is "rich in mercy" (Ephesians 2:4). Even the facts of my failure-deserving-judgment are met by God's mercy. Astoundingly, His great kindness manifest

glory, honor, and

through this trait of His nature makes it possible for righteousness and peace to "kiss each other" (Psalm 85:10). And as though that weren't amazing enough, Scripture tells us that the Father's mercy "endures forever!" (This is stated dozens of times, and more than twenty all at once in one chapter of the Bible—Psalm 136.)

With God, "mercy" isn't an uncertain option but rather a divine certainty. It is guaranteed compassion. It is paid-in-full forgiveness at the specific moment and point of need (Hebrews 4:16).

In His wisdom, He frequently chooses to meet our needs by showing His love toward us through the hands and hearts of others. We have all been at the mercy of love—a love which the "Father of mercies" (2 Corinthians 1:3) has sired in our hearts. We have been the helpless recipients of an outflow of merciful thoughtfulness and kindness. We have been blessed beyond our capacities to produce adequate words of thanksgiving to those who have prayed, cared, called, given, cooked, helped, encouraged . . . and on and on.

His mercy has been great, and He has shown it to each of us. It is wonderful to receive such mercy at the hand of one of His loving children. It is more wonderful still to *be* the hand that touches at the end of His arm that reaches.

That, too, is a privilege born of His mercy.

What to Do With Disappointment

How often do you have to change your plans?

How many times have you counted on something that seemed sure to happen, but then didn't?

How about those situations when you prayed, waited on God, gained an inner witness that He would be working to bring everything about, and then everything was switched?

It's that last issue, I think, that is most troubling: *I just don't understand it. The Lord seemed to have it all together, and then—kablooee!* When that happens, and disappointment begins to clutch at your emotions, what can you do?

This is what helps me:

1. *Don't decide "everything's over!"* Neither a simple glitch in my plans nor an absolute barricade means my life is ended. Our lives are in God's hands—no matter what. Jesus said, "My Father, who has given them [that's us!] to Me, is greater than all; and no one is able to snatch them out of My Father's hand" (John 10:29). Circumstances never—NEVER—change the fundamental absolute undergirding the believer's life: My life is in God's hands.

2. *Let God's peace take command.* The only thing that ever hinders peace is that someone doesn't surrender. So, when upset, dismay, frustration-with-things, or deep disappointment come, "Let the peace of God rule in your hearts" (Colossians 3:15). To surrender to God is never the same as surrendering to the situation—or to whatever

works of hell may be afoot. It is an act of *choice* that over-rules whatever of *chance* seems to be trying your soul, stretching your faith, or overthrowing your confidence. Say, "Lord God Almighty, I give this to You—completely!" And then, with praise upon praise, leave it there (Philippians 4:6,7).

3. *Commit to hope.* There's reason to! For most people you meet, hope is a "cross-my-fingers" kind of thing shot through with guesswork. Instead, for the believer, hope is *divinely assured things that aren't here yet!* Our hope is grounded in unshakable promises. While I may misunderstand God's timing, God's ways, and even wonder about God's presence, He doesn't change: "It is impossible for God to lie . . . [thus we] have fled for refuge to lay hold of the hope set before us. This hope we have as an anchor of the soul, both sure and steadfast" (Hebrews 6:18,19).

4. *Let go of any need to "look good."* Much of our disappointment is rooted in our fears, and among the greatest of those is the fear that our change in plans or our apparent setback will embarrass us before other people. "You don't know what you're doing!" someone may say. And there may be others who question your relationship with God or fly in the face of your disappointment with even more discouraging remarks. But don't allow the need to appear in "perfect control" of your life and circumstances put you in the position of trying to justify everything. Don't mind saying, "Maybe I was wrong," even if you're sure you weren't—but just don't understand it all yet.

5. *Praise the Lord—quietly.* Give yourself over to the spirit of faith—that's the Holy Spirit. But don't paste on a fake smile and give forth with the religious, "Praise the Lord anyway!" But *do* praise Him—do stand in faith! We cannot see the way God is going to work where we are right now, but be sure, *He will:* " 'For the mountains shall depart and the hills be removed, but My kindness shall not depart from you, nor shall My covenant of peace be

removed,' says the LORD, who has mercy on you" (Isaiah 54:10).

Disappointment is changed by altering only one letter—the first one—to "H." Turn *dis*appointment into *His* appointment. Then, stand still and watch Him keep His appointment with your destiny.

P.S. And read Romans 8:31-39!

On a Rock In a Hard Place

We stood on a little bridge spanning the trickling creek. The calm flow of water in late September in no way resembled the surgings and torrents that gush through that site when the spring thaws come to Yosemite.

Looking downstream, Anna and I observed the mighty boulders scattered along the length of the stream bed, mute evidence of the explosive power of that creek at floodtime. As we did, I mused over a young redwood tree, standing right in the middle of the creek. On a slight, rocky rise, around which its gnarled root system clung, it had somehow found a way to begin its life on that perilous perch.

That it had begun didn't surprise me, in spite of the difficult granite footing, for seedlings are born by the millions and swept away in the flush of the spring tides. What *did* surprise me, was that it had survived. I wondered how that happened there in the middle of a stream. If the surging waters hadn't washed it away, surely the crashing boulders should have crushed it.

But there it was. Tall. Serene. Probably ten to twelve years old, and clearly destined to stand for decades, if not centuries, to come.

I drew a conclusion on my own.

That tree's survival was related to a drought.

I can't prove that, but there is no way in the world the young tree could have survived its setting if there had not been a two or three year period when the spring thaw was light. It was obvious that during the tree's infant existence, the clawing fingers of the creek-become-river didn't reach as high or pull as hard. The lower waters kept the annual floods and the rolling boulders from threatening its life.

But another factor came into play with the drought.

The tree's roots searched more deeply for their supply. The dry spell was a blessing which not only allowed for survival, but which created the setting for firmer anchoring against the springtimes ahead. The rushings of the stream would be withstood because of roots sunk deep during dry times.

Then I thought about God . . . and about His providence. I thought about the fact that notwithstanding human interpretations about "chance," "fate," "luck," and the sundry other terms of human incredulity, the Creator's hand had planted that tree. I thought about God's life and breath establishing that seed. About His foreseeing my wife and me standing on that little bridge someday, learning from His textbook of creation.

And I praised Him.

I said, "Thank You, Lord, for the dry times in my soul—times when I think I would prefer surgings, but times when You are calling me deeper, deeper into a more thorough grasp of Your love and sustaining grace toward me." And I thought of the verse: "He shall be like a tree planted . . ." (Psalm 1:3).

Wherever you are and whatever seems to be lacking around you, go deeper. You aren't there by accident. He has you there on purpose.

You'll not only survive by His grace, you'll thrive.

One of my favorite sport-quotes came from the light-heavyweight boxer, Willie Pastrano. After being knocked down several times by José Torres, Pastrano found himself staring up at the ring doctor.

"Do you know where you are?" the doctor asked.

"You better believe I know where I am," Willie replied. "I'm in Madison Square Garden, getting beat up!"

As funny as that incident strikes me, there's nothing funny about getting bashed up and pushed around. The boxer stepping onto the canvas well may expect it, but when you come to the end of a day and have taken your lumps—and often from sources you never imagined or expected—it's hard to smile.

I don't know if you feel "beat-up" right now, but for those who might, I want to recommend an address for cut-and-bruise treatment.

It's called the Mercy Seat.

In the Old Testament, it's the place God provided for people who had been beaten up by life—failures, sinning, brokenness, wounds. The focal point of God's answer to human need was the Mercy Seat. And He invited people to approach it, saying, "I'll meet you there."

In the New Testament, He makes it even more personal, saying, "You are not dealing with Someone who cannot understand your weaknesses. You are coming to a Savior who has been tempted in every way you have; and though He never sinned He understands you and urges you boldly—yes, boldly—to approach the Throne of Grace (that's "the Mercy Seat") where you can obtain mercy and find grace to help in your time of need" (Hebrews 4:15-16, my paraphrase).

Do you feel "beat-up-on"? It's smart to admit it if you do. And it's even smarter to come to the right place for help.

> Is there a heart o'er-bound by sorrow?
> Is there a life weighed down by care?
> Come to the Cross, each burden bearing,
> All your anxiety, leave it there.

> All your anxiety, all your care,
> Bring to the mercy seat, leave it there.
> Never a burden that He cannot bear,
> Never a friend like Jesus.[2]

Come to Him. He's not just the Great Physician, He's the Cut-and-Bruise Specialist.

lift up on high

Birthdays

I think you'd love the way we celebrate birthdays at the Hayford house.

In fact, we have *big* birthday parties here *five* times a year. With our four kids who are married, their spouses, eight grandkids, Anna, myself, and great-grandma Hayford, there's a total of nineteen birthdays to celebrate each year.

We accomplish all of that celebration, however, in five big events. We cluster groups of birthdays, and have celebrations in January, April, June, September, and December. Of course, each family celebrates each individual's birthday on their own and on the actual day. Our "cluster" celebrations are just for family fun.

And we *do* have fun!

It's a riot watching all the smaller grandkids play together. It's exhilarating to go out in the driveway and shoot baskets with my sons and the older grandboys. It's delightful to watch the explosion of paper and ribbons as the presents are opened. And it's most ful-FILL-ing to enjoy the feast as everyone brings his or her share of the meal, and we experience a smorgasbord of salads, hot dishes, and—of course—the cake!

Beginning last year, I started feeling a deep sense of the importance of communicating to people the significance of their birth. Such an emphasis may not seem important to you or me. We may have been raised in a family climate of love and support. We may have lived in a home where, early on, we were taught our worth and significance—with big birthday celebrations that illustrated the point!

But it is increasingly true of our society that fewer and fewer people are brought up in a family atmosphere which cultivates a sense of worth. More and more people tend to feel like "cosmic accidents." Many dear souls have a background of being treated as "problems," as "unwanted arrivals," as "unplanned-and-therefore-unspecial" beings.

My heart throbs to do what I can by God's grace, in every way possible, to instill in the heart of every person I can reach an abiding sense of significance. There is nothing like the truth of God's Word to settle this issue; to create an internal sense of this fact: Every person is a case of "planned parenthood"—*God planned you!* Whatever else may have seemed to be happenstance, there were no surprises in heaven when either you or I arrived on earth!

Because some were born illegitimately, with deformity, or conceived in less than desired circumstances, people draw the conclusion that God wasn't involved in the process. But listen: the fact that God may not have willed the *way* a person came into the world, does not mean He has not planned a *purpose* for that individual. Long before anyone is conceived, God's purpose for that LIFE is foreseen:

> *Just as He chose us in Him before the foundation of the world, that we should be holy and without blame before Him in love, having predestined us to adoption as sons by Jesus Christ to Himself, according to the good pleasure of His will (Ephesians 1:4-5).*

The Bible doesn't teach that our *way* of arrival on earth was programmed by God in some computer-like plan of a predestined order. But it *does* teach that HE

KNEW WE'D BE BORN, and that HE CARED ENOUGH TO PLAN A PURPOSE FOR EACH OF US—INDIVIDU-ALLY!

In short, Father-God is the one who planned for you and me. He's the *Parent* who is eternally committed to working for the fulfillment of His purpose in us, and giving all grace and power from day to day that His plan for us may be fulfilled.

And birthdays? They ought to be an annual celebration of God's plan for you . . . a new opportunity to declare His blessing upon you for another year.

Let's make a big deal out of these worthy celebrations. Let's take time to give cards and presents and notes and words and greetings . . . and certainly a hug or two (or ten!). But let's incorporate those expressions with statements of high and holy truth: The Lord God has created every one of us with magnificent purpose and infinite worth.

If it's your birthday, take the Lord with you on a walk or out for an ice cream cone. Enjoy the present of His presence and the light of His smile. He's glad you're alive . . . and so am I.

How Long the Night

How long the night? I do not know, and
    God in mercy does not show me how . . .
      How long the night.
How soon the harvest? I can't tell, and
    He whose sun and rain will swell the
      seed—He does not say.
How long until? How long to wait? How
    long before at Heaven's gate
      will justice come?
Pray, Watchman, say, when comes the dawn?
    My hope, my faith are nearly gone.
      How long the night?

An answer comes now through the shade;
    The voice is firm—I am afraid
      I've tempted God.
Have I been rash? What will He say?
    He speaks, His words my fear allay,
      "The Day is sure.
"The day is sure, my child beloved,
    The darkness covering above you
      cannot last.
"Would you could see it from my side,
    it thins; it cannot long abide the light
      I pour your way.
It comes—the Day!
    "And do not fear the seed won't grow
      beneath the sod where it was sown

It's growing now.
    "The harvest comes, it will not wait, tho'
        it seems long, it's growing late,
I tell you true,
    The harvest comes,
        I promise you."

O Lord, my eyes can only see the
    earth-side shape of things to be,
        And tho' I cry,
I now confess Your Word, my own, and
    fix my heart on You alone, who
        speak to me.

I say,
The Day is sure, the night will fade, the
    harvest—tho' it seems delayed—
        will surely come.
My eyes shall see it, all around, the light,
    the wheat upon the ground,
        When morning comes,
        When harvest comes,
    My eyes shall see.[3]

MARCH

Remembrance

who died, now

Nobody wanted Him;
  no one remained.
They only taunted Him
  when His Cross was stained
With the blood freely given
  for a world enchained.
Nobody, nobody, no one but nobody came.

glorified, King

A Very Strange Easter to You!

I have to chuckle at the number of people who want God to be predictable.

It is "not fair" for God to act suddenly, powerfully, dramatically, or conclusively. These folks would have Him prepackage life in molded plastic wrapping, so that they could look at each issue *before* the fact, and decide whether they want to embrace it or not.

Easter is God's answer to this fear-trait.

In the resurrection of His Son, God is making an explosive declaration that we're not only ignorant of His boundless power, we're also ignorant of the limitless creativity of His *method*.

Who would have expected the resurrection?

The answer in Scripture is clear: No one. Even those Jesus told specifically and clearly in advance were caught off guard.

How could he have stated it any plainer?

> *"The Son of Man . . . will be delivered to the Gentiles and will be mocked and insulted and spit upon. And they will scourge Him and put Him to death. And the third day He will rise again"* (Luke 18:31-33).

of all Kings.

He told them, but they didn't listen. We're all that way. We'll only hear of the expected. We may wish for or dream of the unexpected, but if God tells us it's going to happen, we either doubt it or fear it. We think He might not do what He has said. Or we're afraid He will.

And He says He will. Listen.

For the LORD shall rise up as in mount Perazim, he shall be wroth as in the valley of Gibeon, that he may do his work, his strange work; and bring to pass his act, his strange act (Isaiah 28:21, KJV).

This promise is a potent commentary on God's unpredictability. The word "strange" doesn't mean "bizarre" or "weird." The Hebrew word used in this text means *unusual*, or coming from an unexpected source.

The examples given by the prophet illustrate the point. Mount Perazim refers to the occasion in which God gave David a dramatic victory by breaking forth like a flood tide over the adversaries he faced. The valley of Gibeon refers to the day the sun stood still in the heavens to afford Joshua and his army the opportunity to conclude their triumph over their enemies. Both cases speak of victory in adversity.

And both were strange. Unusual. Unpredictable.

As unpredictable as winning a battle you don't actually fight, in which the enemy is swept from your path by a tidal wave of God's power rolling out ahead of you.

As unpredictable as the sun standing still. That's strange, friend, strange.

But not as strange as the dead rising.

That's the strangest of all. Empty graves are in a league of their own. Jesus' resurrection categorically *excludes* any hopelessness in any situation and *includes* anyone who opens to His life-gift. This is something more than life beyond death; it is life beyond hope. God's declaration that He shall "rise up" and work an unusual deliverance is ultimately confirmed and manifested in the resurrection of Jesus. When hope fades, life-expectancy can rise again. When shadows crowd you, expect the unexpected.

Easter is the evidence that such expectations are reasonable.

I came across a phenomenon sometime back; a peculiar expression by some sincere Christians who felt it was "unspiritual to make a big thing out of Easter."

In fact, they reacted so much to the traditional practices of big crowds, much music, high rejoicing, and dressing-up that they refused even to go to church on Easter (though they did go most of the year).

While I didn't agree with them, I wasn't particularly irritated. I took it all with a shrug of the shoulders and a takes-all-kinds-to-each-his-own allowance for their peculiarity.

But the more I thought about this, the more I became convinced that they were not only wrong, but they were victims of a deadly kind of reactionary spirit. It stirred me to press all the more for a bold, loud, forthright, festive, and celebrative Easter. Why do I recommend this sort of thinking?

First, because it's consistent with the Bible.

The angel at the tomb said, "Go quickly and tell His disciples" (Matthew 28:7). The obvious reason is to spread the word. *Tell* everybody. And be quick about it. Don't sit on Good News. This is a day above all days!

Then on Easter night, after their first encounter with their resurrected Master, the Word says, "Then the disciples were *glad* when they saw the Lord" (John 20:20).

The whole spirit of the day is to spread the word to more and more. Crowds are the idea! And gladness should be *everywhere*. It's in the Book!

Second, because it's simply logical.

Since death has been vanquished, the more lively our celebration the more appropriate to the occasion. No wonder so many people dress up with new clothes on Easter. While some may attack that practice as some sort of "carnal parade," I hold that new Easter outfits are just one more way to say, "New life is here, and I'm celebrating the newness!" Jesus had new clothes on Easter, too!

Third, because a "big" Easter should summon prayerful preparation among the Lord's people.

At least two reasons make this appropriate:

• The Good Friday lead-in to Easter's weekend is a heart-sobering time of humbling our souls and reflecting on the Cross of Christ—the price of our salvation.

• Easter Sunday is a unique occasion to invite people to church and to Christ. People will more likely visit with you on this day than any other . . . and we ought to pray for their spiritual openness.

Fourth, because the very thought of the resurrection should fill the skies with our songs of triumph!

Jesus Christ has burst forth from the tomb and the open door of the grave shouts like a song-filled mouth—"Christ is risen! Rejoice! Rejoice!"

If that doesn't make you want to celebrate, this Easter ask for a resurrection of your own!

Unto Jesus he a

More Than a Savior

Filled with drama and emotion, the biblical book of Ruth tells the story of a young woman who lost everything but her will to trust in God. It concludes with her marriage to a man named Boaz, whose principal role in Ruth's life is defined in a single word: *redeemer*.

The purpose of this piece of history being included in the Bible may have been to describe the entrance of a Gentile woman into the ancestral bloodline of the Messiah. But students of the Bible see an even grander lesson.

Here is great insight into God's ways of dealing with ruined people. Here is the picture of the "kinsman-redeemer"—a role and relationship God gave under the Old Covenant in order to help us understand His ways under the New.

The kinsman-redeemer law stated that if someone lost his possessions through the death of a loved one, another one of his "kin" could volunteer to repossess that which was lost (Leviticus 25:24,25). The kinsman's "redeemer" role was fulfilled in two ways: (1) He had to acknowledge his relationship with the one who had suffered loss; and (2) he had to pay the required price for the recovery of what had been lost.

In the case of Boaz's redeeming actions toward Ruth, he became both a rescuer and a restorer. Ruth was a foreigner and alien in a new cultural environment. Boaz received this disenfranchised widow as his wife and

glory, honor and

68

graciously secured her future through restoration of property she otherwise would have lost.

The power of this story transcends its immediate beauty, emotion, and historical significance. Its force emerges in its dynamic picture of what Jesus Christ has done and will do for everyone who puts his or her trust in Him. Jesus is the Savior, but He is even more than that! He is more than a Forgiver of our sins. He is even more than our Provider of eternal life. He is our Redeemer! He is the One who is ready to recover and restore what the power of sin and death has taken from us.

It is a mighty truth, worthy of our deepest understanding. Here's how He does it.

HE ACKNOWLEDGES US.

The kinsman-redeemer pictured in the Old Testament had to step forward in open declaration of his relationship to the individual who had been shamed, embarrassed, or ruined by loss or failure. Just as Boaz responded to Ruth's appeal for help, the Lord Jesus Christ has fully come to us as a Kinsman. "The Word became flesh and dwelt among us" (John 1:14). God became "kin" to man! He took upon Himself the form of a servant and was made in the likeness of men (Philippians 2:7), fully demonstrating His willingness to associate with us—even though we have sinned against Him. He who never sinned at all was willing to be invested with our sin in order to become our Sin-Bearer and Savior (2 Corinthians 5:21).

But having become "one of us," He went one step further. He personally acknowledges a relationship to each of us: "He is not ashamed to call each of us His brothers—His sisters—His very own family" (Hebrew 2:11; my paraphrase). None of us has failed too badly or fallen too far to remove us from His willingness to identify with us. He has become our Kinsman, and He is ready to claim association with any who will come to Him.

HE PAID THE PRICE.

The word "redeem," as used in the Bible, describes "a price that has been paid." In the pawn shop usage of the term, a broker gives a "redemption ticket" that a person may use to reclaim something he has sold for far less than its worth.

This "pawn shop" image holds a powerful lesson. It provides a dramatic picture of the way sin works in human lives; tempting us to sell out for less than God's promised blessing, and leaving us with little or nothing as a reward. Yet, as with the rules of the "pawn shop redemption," recovery occurs when a greater price is paid for the redeeming of what had been "sold cheap" and lost. And that is what Jesus did as Savior:

> *In Him we have redemption through His blood, the forgiveness of sins, according to the riches of His grace (Ephesians 1:7).*

> *You were not redeemed with corruptible things, like silver or gold . . . but with the precious blood of Christ (1 Peter 1:18, 19).*

Everything Jesus offers of new life, new hope, and new possibilities is guaranteed to us on the basis of a total and complete payment.

HE BRINGS FULL RECOVERY.

Few realize the thrilling truth that Christ's payment for our "redemption" involves an ongoing, continual process of recovery! The significance of this provision is clearly apparent when we assess the destructive impact of sin and failure on the human personality.

How many have suffered loss because of sin!

So many have been injured, broken, and damaged.

People are so often left as emotional, physical, and mental casualties through human failure.

The failure may not even be one's own. Damaged people are often the result of someone else's neglect, exploitation, or violation. On the other hand, the loss may be the individual's own just due, resulting from conscious rebellion or defiance toward what he or she knew to be right. Nevertheless, the wreckage wrought in any of our lives may be mended as surely as the sin may be forgiven.

The precious truth of Jesus' power as Redeemer is that He has a plan and an ability to progressively restore the broken parts of human experience and to reproduce a whole person. His salvation is not only an act of forgiveness, it is also a progressive action of redemption. He not only meets us at the moment of our new birth, but His saving life generates a momentum which can bring us into the fullness of restored life and joy.

There is no dearer truth in the Word of God than this: Christ is "able to save to the uttermost those who come to God through Him" (Hebrews 7:25). That simply means that in the recovery process, there is no distance too great for Him to bring us.

God said to the farmers of ancient Israel, "I will restore to you the years that the swarming locust has eaten" (Joel 2:25). In those words He prophesies a promise answering our present need as well. Whatever has been decayed or destroyed, He is our Restorer—Recoverer—Redeemer!

Whatever your loss, pain, failure, or brokenness, Jesus Christ is fully capable of bringing about change unto full restoration. Just as His resurrection power brings new life, His redemption power brings new hope. He is able, for He's more than a Savior! He's your Redeemer who promises that He will give "beauty for ashes, the oil of joy for mourning" (Isaiah 61:3).

So just as you gave Him your heart and received Him as Savior, give Him your life's broken pieces—receive Him as Redeemer. Give Him time to work a full redemptive recovery in each part of your life. Let these promises be set in motion as in childlike faith you receive His commitment to restore everything sin has damaged, lost, or ruined.

Begin now to praise Him! You will discover that worshiping Him in this light leads out of the darkness of all despair over sin's effect and aftermath. Let redemptive power and life flow as you praise Jesus Christ—your Savior and your Redeemer!

Easter A New Order

The chaotic, the run-amok, and the pointless are traits of our time.

Consider the relentless parade of activities, the incessant flood of mail, the endless ringing of telephones, the stream of requirements, adjustments in procedure, refinements of policy that flow to you from your superior at work.

Students face assignment piled on assignment.

All of us endure a barrage of information, entertainment, and miscellany that keeps our eyes glued to the TV tube—lest we miss something. A dozen new magazines a week suggest you subscribe to keep abreast of what's *really* happening.

The modern American preoccupation with being contemporary, informed, and socially "with it" drives most of us toward a life of whirlwind confusion. Gadgets expedite the performance of all our essential duties. Speed-read courses help us weather the storm of print sweeping upon us. Plans to systematize your day, week, month, year, and other "hurry-up-and-get-it-done-right" techniques are upon us ad infinitum.

In the midst of it all . . . the police whistle of my soul screams its shrill command—HALT!

It is only as I stand there, mentally gasping for breath, that I discover how tired I have become . . . how much I want to stop. Not to stop living, but to stop rushing. Not to retreat from reality, but to reenter life.

Looking up, I discover where the call of my soul has brought me to a complete stop: at Jesus' empty tomb.

Step in with me, and as we rejoice in the triumph of His resurrection, let us learn from one detail there. The Gospel of John records Peter and John's arrival at the tomb.

> *So they both ran together, and the other disciple out-ran Peter and came to the tomb first. And he, stooping down and looking in, saw the linen cloths lying there; yet he did not go in. Then Simon Peter came, following him, and went into the tomb; and he saw the linen cloths lying there, and the handkerchief that had been around His head, not lying with the linen cloths, but folded together in a place by itself. Then the other disciple, who came to the tomb first, went in also; and he saw and believed (John 20:4-8).*

Among the powerful resurrection evidence reported is the fact that Peter and John found the grave clothes Jesus had left, folded, lying neatly wrapped. What would elude the casual reader cannot but impress the thoughtful student. This piece of evidence requires the intellectually honest to rule out at least two explanations for the empty tomb which skeptics propose: (1) Grave thieves? They aren't that neat. (2) A buried-alive-swooned-but-didn't-die Christ "struggling in weakness from the tomb"? He wouldn't bother.

But more than that, the carefully arranged grave clothes and the linen napkin that had enwrapped Jesus' head suggest a new order at the Resurrection. The explosion of life that burst the bonds of death has a simple system to it. Step inside the closed tomb, and with your imagination watch the body of Christ begin to breathe. See the Son of God sit up, remove the head-wrap, and methodically disrobe Himself from the cloth-chains which symbolize man's final futility. The garments are neatly placed at the spot where He removes each. And as you look, you see Him clothed by garments not of earthly origin—garments which will be worn later that day as He comforts a tearful woman, as He hikes to Emmaus with two troubled disciples, and that evening as He dines with the men closest to Him.

So many applications are there for our understanding. But rather than draw them all, just pray with me, would you?

Lord Jesus, let the new order of life which You opened to me reign over me. Clothe me with Your unhurried, not-stampeded-by-urgency mindedness. Let the powerful simplicity of Your order and control characterize my heart, my home, and my hopes.

Mandatory Nine Count

I can't number the times I have wished God would hurry up . . . with an answer to my prayer . . . with a bailout in the middle of my muddle . . . with a fresh sense of His working in my life.

But there is one well-established principle in the Scriptures, and it is dramatically demonstrated in Jesus' experience.

You can't rush a resurrection.

Matthew's Gospel records no less than three times that Jesus clearly prophesied that He would be killed by His adversaries and that He would rise again (16:21, 17:23, 20:19). He not only stated precisely that it would be the third day, but He predicated His resurrection upon an Old Testament type: the third-day deliverance of Jonah from the belly of the great fish (Matthew 12:40).

These advance notices of His resurrection are forceful arguments for Jesus' sense of purpose and power. They also offer a valuable lesson for you and me. If I am walking in the simple path of God's will for me, *I can never be conquered by anything.* I may be down, but I'm not out. He will get me up again, and He says when it will be . . . on the count of three.

Have you ever seen boxers, flattened by their opponent, try to scramble to their feet too quickly? Rather than taking the nine-count, using the time to recover their equilibrium, they attempt a quick bounce-back. It's almost as though they're trying to convince themselves, the crowd, and their opponent that they weren't *really* hurt. Somehow, a downed boxer's identity seems wrapped in his ability to show a "can't hurt me" facade, when, in fact, his hurried rising—I've seen it often—leaves him wobbling, staggering, and open prey for a quick kill at the hand of his competitor.

Consider with me, friend: If Jesus could have called for angels to spare Him the suffering of the Cross (Matthew 26:53), don't you know that He could have called for an early deliverance from death? The message of His submission to the Father's timing as well as the Father's plan is profound in its application to your life and mine.

lift up on high

Don't attempt a humanly energized "bounce-back" from those circumstantial "knock-downs" you encounter. God has His own kind of "mandatory nine-count": it's a third-day rising for everyone who will wait for His moment of miracle deliverance.

"Easy to say, Pastor Jack, but I've waited longer than three days, or three weeks, or three months . . . in fact, more than three years. What about my resurrection?"

I hear you. And I know the pain often wrapped in that kind of inquiry. But the answer is in a return question: "Have you entrusted everything concerning your case to Jesus?" If you have, then the entire matter is sealed and delivered . . . in His resurrection.

The message is this: As surely as Jesus rose on time, your triumph will be on schedule also.

Lazarus's schedule probably seemed a day late to him, too.

I Believe In The Resurrection

I believe in the resurrection of Jesus Christ, the Son of God; that He personally, physically, and actually died, and on the third day rose again according to the Scriptures. I believe that by His resurrection He declared His deity and announced His conquest of death and hell, and that all who believe this in their heart may be saved.

Because I believe this, I confess with my mouth the Lord Jesus and worship Him whom I glorify as the Son of God, risen from the grave and ascended upon high in triumph above all the powers of darkness.

I believe in the resurrection of the just, that at Christ's coming we shall all be changed into the likeness of His glorious, resurrected body. I believe that we shall receive eternal, physical bodies which shall not be subject to decay, and that in that glorified state we shall forever be with and serve the living God.

Because I believe this, I live life in hope of the resurrection, without fear of death and without bondage to the endless grievings of those who have no such hope.

I believe in the resurrection of all mankind, that on the last day every creature shall stand before the throne of God and give account for the deeds done in the body. I believe that by His death and resurrection, Christ Jesus has made it possible for every man to anticipate that day with joy, but that all those resistant to His Lordship shall experience endless judgment in bodies intended to know eternal blessing rather than eternal shame.

Because I believe this, I walk in faith and holy sobriety, knowing that my motives as well as my deeds, my thoughts as well as my words constitute the substance of eternal values which I either serve or shirk and according to which I shall be judged before the loving and righteous Father.

With such an expectation as this, I can walk in praise to a resurrected Savior who has not only given me an eternal hope, but who can fill me with an eternal quality of life and power to live daily in the resources of His victory.

Supporting Scriptures:

John 19:1-20:31; 1 Corinthians 15:1-8; Psalm 16:8-11; Romans 1:4; 10:9, 10; Ephesians 1:19-21.

1 Corinthians 15:51-58; 1 Thessalonians 4:13-18; 1 John 3:2; Philippians 3:20, 21; Job 19:26.

Revelation 20:11-15; Luke 16:19-31; 1 Corinthians 3:12-15; 2 Corinthians 5:9-10.

Magnify, come

The Resurrection Dimension

When Jesus said, *"Because I live, you will live also,"* He was declaring a new dimension of life available to any who will receive Him and His.

Most believers in Jesus live an inferior quality of life simply because they have never come to terms with His full offer. Christ the Lord, the resurrected Son of God, has made available to us both forgiveness of sins *and* fullness of life. Forgiveness comes when we receive Him as Savior; fullness comes when we receive the offer of His life.

The Good Friday dimension of life says, "Christ died for my sins." I believe that, and I receive the payment He made for my sin. I acknowledge the penalty He suffered as a result of my wrongdoing. But that does not teach the full measure of provision which God has made possible through the redeeming work of our Lord. There is a Resurrection dimension of life also, and it is wrapped in the words of Romans 1:

> . . . *The gospel of God . . . concerning His Son Jesus Christ our Lord, who was born of the seed of David according to the flesh, and declared to be the Son of God with power, according to the Spirit of holiness, by the resurrection from the dead (vv. 1, 3-4).*

This passage clearly tells us that it was through the power of the Holy Spirit that Jesus was raised from the dead.

That Man who strode forth from the tomb twenty centuries ago is still speaking today: "Because I live, you will live also (John 14:19).

Glorify Christ Jesus,

Look closely, now. Those words are not only a promise of an endless life in the glory of God's presence, they hold a guarantee of a *present life* in the glory of God's power. Jesus is telling you and me we can move out of the limits of mere human resources for living, into the dimension of the Holy Spirit's resources for our living.

Today I invite you where Christ invites you: to live in the resurrection resources of the Spirit-filled life. Romans 8:11 says this is the present and fulfilling potential that awaits each of us who will receive Christ's life-power (fullness) as well as His love-power (forgiveness): "If, then, the Spirit of Him who raised Jesus from the dead dwells in you, then He who raised Christ Jesus from the dead will through the Spirit that dwells in you also make your mortal bodies live" (MLB).

Step to a new plateau! Let's stand together in the full possibilities of Jesus' life working in us. The Resurrection dimension is no twilight zone of mysticism, but a real, practical, and powerful dynamic for life in the here and now.

A Shepherd's Call To New Heights

Spring is the season the shepherd calls the sheep to leave the lowlands and begin to climb the heights. Winter snows past, the mountains spread their carpet of verdant beauty. Fresh grass, sprays of flowers, and blossoming trees beckon upward.

Come, My flock—rich feasting and fulfilling growth await if you follow Me to the heights.

> Hear the upward call of the Master;
> Lift your eyes and you will see
> New horizons appear,
> and the challenge is clear,
> Come and climb the heights with me.

> Never let your heart be shackled
> by affections earthly bound.
> Follow Christ today
> up the narrow way
> That leads to higher ground.[4]

Lent is a synonym for spring, an old English word for this bright season of newness. It is also a religious term which denotes the *lenten* observances of self-denial which many Christians have traditionally practiced during the forty days preceding Easter. Like many traditions, Lent has suffered the decay that infests and eventually destroys valid habits when they are not understood—or not observed in spiritually vital ways.

I strongly believe that in approaching Easter and the glorious days preceding—Palm Sunday, Maundy Thursday, and Good Friday—we should require something special of ourselves. These days should not go by as ordinary. The classical term "Holy Week" may sound archaic and coldly liturgical. But what our Lord Jesus did in those eight days has forever changed history—and each of our lives.

Therefore, Jesus Himself is the focus of the summons I issue as I call you *upward*—to climb the heights, to move on to rich pastures in His purpose as *He* calls us all.

And this is the way I am calling:

ONE: Pick a book of Scripture, preferably one of the Gospels, and make a commitment to read it all the way through in these pre-Easter weeks. Don't be afraid of what the Holy Spirit can do in you as the *truth* makes you free.

TWO: Make a point of inviting at least two couples or singles into your home—or out for coffee—during these lenten days. Make the attempt to reach out to people in the body who are not part of your usual circle of friends.

THREE: Set aside the ten days leading to Easter as *TEN DAYS OF TRIUMPH.* Allow Him to help you focus on one personal discipline that you will resolve to practice every day until Easter Sunday.

The life of resurrection victory awaits us all. More is intended to blossom this springtime than just the trees. Let's all go upward and forward together.

Raised by hate upon a hill, stark there stands a Cross of wood,
Look, the Man they take and kill is the Lamb, the Son of God.
See the blood now freely flow; "It is finished," hear Him cry!
Who can understand or know: death has won; yet death will die.

All is well, all is well,
Through Christ our Conq'rer,
All is well
All is well, all is well,
Through Christ our Conq'erer
All is well.

Slashing wounds now scar the Lamb, blemish free until
    He's slain,
Hammer blows into His hand thunder forth again, again.
See His body raised in scorn, see the spear now split His
    side!
Yet the vict'ry shall be won by this Man thus crucified.

Look! The Cross now raised on high—symbol of Christ's
    reign above.
Cow'ring demons fear and fly, driv'n before the flame of
    love.
All of hell is mystified; Satan thought this hour his gain.
See God's wisdom glorified: death destroyed in Jesus'
    name.

Here is hope in hopelessness, here is joy where all is pain.
Here a fount of righteousness flows to all who make their
    claim.
Come and drink here, come and live. Come and feast on
    life and peace.
In the Cross God's all He gives, in the Cross is full release.

Tow'ring o'er all history stands the Cross of Christ the
    King.
Crossroad of all destiny, at the Cross is ev'rything.
See here death hung on a Cross, see self slain upon a tree,
See disease and ev'ry loss overthrown through Calvary!

    All is well, all is well,
    Through Christ our Conq'rer,
    All is well
    All is well, all is well,
    Through Christ our Conq'erer
    All is well.[5]

APRIL
Growth

of all Kings.

I've got the life of God in me,
The power that made all the universe
  with just a word
Has come to live in me
  abundantly.
I've got the life of God in me.

April Fools

Some explain April Fools' Day as a relic of the Roman festival *Cerealia*, held at the beginning of April.

The mythology behind the observance is interesting. Prosperina, playing in the spring-sprouted daffodils fresh upon the Elysian meadows, is kidnaped by Pluto and carried off to the underworld. Her mother, Ceres, upon seeking her, forever chases the echoes of her daughter's screams, but never finds her.

I inquired into this tidbit of mythical lore today because I am persuaded that our culture's holiday and fun-day observances will always have something to teach us . . . if we program them to do so.

I hold no stock with those who expend their energy debunking special days, tirelessly warning people that the observance of such-and-such a day is "a surrender to paganism." Frankly, I have difficulty being patient with a mentality that is half witch hunt and half sour grapes. I prefer to enjoy the simple and innocent delights of our culture's calendar (insofar as the dates can be simply and innocently observed!) and to program those dates in my mind to make them serve me. I do that by linking them with annual reminders of some practical truth in the Word of God.

Ceres' pursuit of her kidnaped daughter is an interesting point, for Pluto, in Roman mythology, is the equivalent of the "son of Satan." The mother's quest for her daughter, deluded and detoured by the echoes of her screams, suggests an equally bewildering quest common to many people in our world.

Springtime awakens in nearly everyone the longing for agelessness, the quest for romance, and the search for some fountain of youth. The renewal of the landscape gives rise to the human wish for an endless succession of fulfilling years. The season produces a string of pathetic human attempts to recapture lost youth:

- the underdressed matron or the overly made-up woman;

- the forty-to-fiftyish male ogling disinterested girls, thinking his clever banter can somehow reverse the clock;

- the macho man whose quest to prove his youthful manliness concludes at a Jacuzzi nursing strained muscles;

- women overspending time and money at health and beauty spas, attempting to meet society's standards of glamour (when a few simple exercises and a little self-denial would shape and release the loveliness wrought in them by the Creator's hand).

It's springtime, and happily so. But I've determined April First shall serve me as a reminder of the blessing of increased years. Aging holds no fear for those who drink at the fountain of real life in Christ; and springtime speaks of resurrection, not dying. As believers in Him who is *Life*, let us refuse at any season to succumb to the haunting cries emanating from the world system, luring us to chase the echoes of elusive youth.

Television, movies, magazine ads, the Avon lady, and the fashion designer all have some positive values to serve. But never let them substitute myths and false images for your true identity. And your age is part of that.

To chase vanished youth is to become an April Fool, no matter what time of year it is.

How Does Your Garden Grow?

When my brother was about four years old, my father helped him plant a little garden in the backyard at our house.

Daddy soon was puzzled by the fact that so many of the little sprouts which had begun so nicely were wilting. He discovered the answer to the mystery a few days later. It seems that my brother—understandably excited over the progress of his garden—had been making daily, unattended, investigative trips to each row. Gently pulling up each of the tender plants, the little guy was examining the roots of each seedling to chart the progress of its growth during the preceding day. He was always careful to place the little sprig back in the soil, but this innocence of inquiry did not neutralize the deadliness of his deeds.

Moral: *If you want to grow, keep your roots in the soil.*

When I was about thirty-five years old, my heavenly Father helped me plant a garden at 14300 Sherman Way, Van Nuys, California. It has grown well. So well that many have been fed by it, including people who don't live in the area. Which is all very well, except that awhile back I sensed some wilting.

glory, honor and

I think I've found out why . . . and what to do about it.

A dozen different influences brought it about, and all as innocent of ill intent as my little brother was. But one incident after another, wherein our growth has been scrutinized, has begun to get in the way of that growth.

People talk about us. We talk among ourselves. Magazine writers phone me for interviews. Christian television abounds with comments on or characters from The Church On The Way. We get written up in newspapers. Institutes study our growth pattern and style of life. The talk goes on and on. Why, it's enough to get us completely impressed with where we go to church.

It's also enough to kill us.

Thankfully, however, our church isn't dead. But I think we can all learn something from this. Your personal growth, my personal growth, the growth of my church, or the growth of your church are all worthy subjects of rejoicing and praise to God. But watch out when such things become the object of your thoughts, conversations, or study. Watch out when you begin collecting the press clippings. Watch out when "growth" becomes an end in itself.

If you find yourself talking "my church this" and "our church that," you had better get your roots back in the soil.

Fast.

Talk about "my Lord Jesus" instead. It's the Holy Spirit, not your pastor, who is the key to growth. It's the Word of God, not a specific Sunday school curriculum or sermon series that is the seed that bears fruit.

Our obedience to biblical principles, not our uniqueness of methods, is fundamental to our spiritual lives. Growing saints in Jesus and seeing reproduction in spiritual life are our responsibilities. If it gets reported on, written up, talked about, photographed, televised, or touted to the moon, that's the business of those who do those things. It isn't yours or mine.

Let's keep our roots in the warm, nourishing soil of simply loving Jesus, praising God, reading and studying the Word, and walking in the Spirit. Counting the fruit and numbering the harvest is the business of the Gardener. Ours is to grow and yield.

A Spring Checklist

I recently sat with a pilot in the cockpit of a private aircraft and watched him prepare for takeoff. After accounting for a list of about two dozen items, he calmly pulled back the stick, and we were airborne.

It was a secure feeling to know that everything had been checked out.

Could it be that God is calling you to new heights of possibility in His purpose for you this day . . . this week . . . this year? Are you cleared for takeoff? If you're *not sure*, I recommend the following checklist to help you determine with confidence that you are "cleared" on these fundamental factors.

Checkpoint #1: Relationships

• Is all clutter of doubt, condemnation, or guilt between Jesus and myself cleared out? Is there a regular flow of one-to-one relationship with Him in prayer, communion, praise, and worship?

• Am I giving adequate attention to all family

relationships? Am I faithfully giving myself to each member of the family? Allowing special time to be with each? Am I forgiving their shortcomings—and seeking their forgiveness for mine?

• Concerning those with whom I work or study: Am I sensitive as an available channel for ministry? What fresh flow of God's love might be released through me? Am I free of all resentment . . . lovelessness?

Checkpoint #2: Maturity

• Am I gaining new points of balance in my understanding? Am I giving God's Spirit opportunity to enlarge my awareness and perspective?

• How do I score in God's mind when it comes to such seemingly diverse principles as "Spirit-filled prayer life" and "fidelity with God's tithe"?

• Where have I been in my private reading and study of God's eternal Word? What points of truth have been opened or deepened in my mind?

Checkpoint #3: My church family

• Am I "in touch" with those things the Holy Spirit is saying to my congregation? Am I hearing Him? Responding? Am I simply a part of the crowd, or am I a contributing part of the family?

• What headway am I making in my growth as an intercessor? Am I growing in prayer for our nation and its leaders? Am I aware of the movement of God's Spirit in different "hot spots" around the world?

• When have I last sought a new acquaintance at more than a surface level of involvement? Am I stagnating with a closing circle of fellowship, or open to and cultivating an expanding circle?

This list, of course, could expand considerably. Maybe yours should, as you say: *Lord, where else do You want me to let a fresh breath of Your life blow out accumulated dust of neglect?*

flow from His

In any case, take time with these. Only He knows what possibilities will open up for you as you climb to new altitudes in His purpose for your life.

The horizons beckon. So does He. Let's respond.

Blessed Are the Flexible

Last year, I received a gift which required doing two things which both irritated me and stoked the fires of my impatience.

First of all, I was required to read instructions and carefully assemble this gift. That was bad enough. But to make matters worse, the instructions were vague—and weighted with technical jargon.

Second, finding a place to put the gift required moving stuff around in my office. I actually had to remove an item which had ornamented my wall for a long time. It had to be put out of the way to make room for this new object.

As the process began to consume more time than I could afford, I found myself clenched-jawed and angry. But even as my ire rose, a still small voice inside me also rose to speak:

You're getting old, Jack. Old and inflexible. You don't want to learn anything new, and you don't want to change anything settled!

Ouch! I winced, and stopped to talk with Jesus.

He was pinpointing a fact of my personal, mundane experience, which—He said to me—held the portent of an attitude which could begin to warp my spiritual life.

I repented. It was good for me.

Gently, the Lord reminded me of His words in Revelation 21:5: "Behold, I make all things new." As I pondered that passage, it struck me that the Lord Jesus was not only making a prophetic promise, He was also asserting an ongoing policy. To keep moving with a living Body—and His Church is supposed to be that—you and I are vulnerable to the spiritual experience of a biological fact. I am told by physicians that the human body renews itself every seven years. All of the body's cells will renew themselves in seven-year cycles—or less.

Through my years of walking with Jesus, I've discovered He keeps me in a permanent state of transition. And I've learned a little about the potential for joy when you allow the Holy Spirit to keep "flex" in your soul.

I don't want to become stodgy. Unshapeable. Inflexible. The ongoing working of the Spirit in my life—and yours—will keep us "hanging loose."

Someone reminded me of those things just the other day. "Blessed are the flexible," my friend said, "for verily, they shall not be broken."

I like that. I might even have someone prepare it in calligraphy and frame it for my wall.

Even if it means moving something else.

Spring Forward!

As a former college administrator, I've come to understand a good deal about people by observing students at springtime.

While clocks "spring forward" on daylight-savings time and romantics sing of blossoms and young love, another human tendency slips in through the back door: *apathy born of weariness.*

"Spring fever" is the classic name for the attrition of energy that settles on us at this season. Some residents of wintry climates link this annual malaise with a "thinning of the blood" as the mercury rises in the thermometer.

I don't think it's quite as exotic as that. I think we're just tired.

Come April, I would watch students begin to fold up. The grind of the academic year, which began a millennium ago in September, had taken its toll. Increased daylight hours beckoned the kids to the parks, the hills, the beach—and, "Hey, why not!?" After seven months of pencil-pushing, a break not only *seemed* justified, it *was* . . . and is!

Problems only come when the spring "break" becomes a runaway from responsibility instead of an appropriate change of pace. College dropout rates at springtime are a notorious problem for many educators.

But beyond campus life, the temptation to a "springtime runaway" is just as much a threat to most of us as it

94

was to the students I served. My people-tending shepherd's task has revealed that this springtime temptation knows no age barriers. The ebb and flow of our adult life tends to follow the academic year, even when we're not in school.

In view of that, I offer three suggestions for fending off the spring slump.

1. Plan a "break" and have a *blast!* Instead of drifting from day to day, fudging on your schedule of duties in the name of "I-deserve-a-break," rally some friends or family and blow it all out! Take some kids and literally "go fly a kite!" Go to the beach, and splash and surf yourself silly. Head for the hills and picnic under the blossoming apple trees. Take a weekend camping trip. Hike yourself into blisters.

Does that sound extreme? Good! It's meant to, because we need to dent our psyche with the fact we did "break," and did it with such diligence that we can say, "That'll hold me until summer vacation."

2. Budget time to keep two "spring cleaning" promises:

"I'm gonna clean out the garage, plant the planter, sort my drawer full of snapshots, reorganize my closets, or paint the _____" (you fill in the blank). Don't labor under an impossible list of dream-goals. It'll drag you to a springtime slump. Just pick two. Set the time for them and *do* them. Then,

3. Spring forward spiritually! Set your sights with mine, will you? Get up early with Jesus the next forty days—even if it's only fifteen minutes before your usual roll-out time. Invest those choice moments praising Him for His presence, seeking His counsel, talking to Him about the brand new day before you.

Walk the pathway to Pentecost with me. Beat back the spring attrition rate. Send the slump slumping.

lift up on high

Big As Life

"I'd just like a little home in the country where life is easy . . . "

"Wouldn't it be nice to have a job with less responsibility . . . "

"Honey, I don't see how we can plan that direction; it's too much . . . "

"It's such a large church, we thought we'd rather attend a smaller . . . "

"Yes, we had the chance for promotion, but Harold thought it better to . . . "

Do you recognize those words? I do. I've said some of them and heard all of them. They're words which characterize our human preference for what poets call "the idyllic." It is the quest for the quiet, the slow, the easy, the undemanding. It is carried out in a scene of tall trees standing sentinel around a small, but comfortable cottage. You can see it, can't you? The wind blowing through the high grass also curls the smoke from the chimney. The clouds on the horizon are purpled by the sunset.

Isn't it beautiful?

Isn't it restful?

Isn't it pointless?

How "big" is life supposed to be?

Are scenes like those visualized above to be places of periodic retreat and rest, or is all of life to be an enchanting

name of Jesus

dream? Honestly, aren't all of us tempted by the presence of duty to permanently flee it?

Of course we are. I resist the pressure of responsibility, and I am troubled by the fact that life seems never to reduce in responsibility—it ceaselessly increases. Hence the load . . . as big as life itself.

What stance do I recommend? Flee, run, resist, wrestle . . . or live?

I vote for life. I say, LIVE.

But live in "the power of an endless life." Hebrews 7:16 relates those magnificent words. They're expressive of the dynamic which Jesus can work inside of anyone who will let Him.

And He keeps making life bigger!

He closes out the possibilities of tiny-ness, pettiness, small-mindedness, non-expectancy, and fear-unto-flight. And while He doesn't move you into the woods, He brings wisdom, discernment, and sound-mindedness to the marketplace of your daily living and thereby . . .

. . . Peace.

Perfect peace. "Peace I leave with you, My peace I give to you; not as the world gives do I give to you. Let not your heart be troubled, neither let it be afraid" (John 14:27). Those are promise-packed words from the Head of the Corporation. He directs that we stay in business, and that we be unafraid of expecting business to increase. He builds quality into the people-products He is recreating to live life to its fullest . . . its largest.

You don't need to be afraid for one moment that the responsibility He brings you will burn out the equipment He's given you.

His life power—endless in quality and quantity—is the resource to guarantee you can more than survive. You can triumph.

Peacefully.

Magnify, come

Lessons While Pulling Weeds

Keeping a lawn and garden can mean an almost daily warfare with weeds. You've got to keep ahead of 'em. If you don't, they can take over with amazing speed.

During a recent weeding session, I began thinking on the way my flesh can provide "ready soil" for carnal ways. How quickly such weeds infest my life, sink their tangled roots, and raise their ugly heads!

As I dug and chopped, pulled and sprayed, I began to tabulate a running inventory on the subject of weeds. I'll leave the list with you for your own meditation and internal gardening.

1. Weeds grow more easily than the plant I want.

2. Weeds often look innocently beautiful while small, but grow dry and ugly when given their place.

3. You can hardly ever remove weeds without getting on your knees.

4. Most weeds can be removed much more easily if they are first soaked with water.

5. Some weeds' roots are so deep it takes the pressing of a blade into the soil to loosen the root and remove it.

6. The removal of weeds by hand requires a delicate

balance of gentleness and firmness: gently loosening, firmly removing.

7.   Weeds spring up most quickly in previously uncultivated soil (i.e., where something new is now happening, but nothing fruitful was growing before).

8.   Careful attention to weeds at the early, critical season prevents multiplication and makes for a lovelier garden.

9.   Weeds often look like the plant you want. It takes discernment to uproot the right sprout.

10.   Weed removal takes patience. If you try to hurry, you can break the root beneath the soil, guaranteeing its reemergence. Don't rush the process.

11.   After the weed is removed, all of the soil's energy may be directed to the intended plant's fruitful growth.

12.   When you are done pulling weeds, you have a deeper appreciation for "the plot."

Now, go back and think about weeding again.

Happy (and holy) gardening!

Life In the family

A slow sunrise on a cloudy day.

We had rolled out of our beds at 4:00 A.M., grabbing oranges and bananas for breakfast as we hurried to the car. After driving fifty miles up a dark highway, we found ourselves huddled together—Anna, the children, and myself—on a lonely promontory, shivering in the wind.

We had come to watch the sunrise over the Grand Canyon.

It took a long time.

The clouds hanging in the east caught and held the light of dawn much longer than usual before the actual rays of the sun struck the painted canyon walls. It was beautiful, and worth planning toward and waiting to see.

But . . . it did take a long time.

Especially for people standing in the cold.

The family memory I've just described might be appropriate for you today for a couple of reasons:

First, as an encouragement to plan unforgettable memories for yourself and your children.

If you, Mom and Dad, don't do this for the little ones growing up under your roof, who will? And for you singles . . . don't forget the ministry of memory-maker is available to you, too. There are nephews and nieces—or ones you might adopt for a few hours—who are just waiting for someone to splash new colors on the canvas of their memories.

Second, as a picture of what "life in the family"—the Body of Christ—is all about.

Reaching out to a wider circle of believers holds the promise of unlocking doors of a full range of New Testament life-and-love-together-in-Jesus for every one of us. But it may be uncomfortable to begin with. It may take longer than we would prefer to draw close to people.

The thought of some kind of "forced closeness" frightens all of us. Rest easy. Love doesn't force, but it does attract and nourish.

The objective? It's grander than the Grand Canyon. Yet the splendor of that magnificent gorge does hint at the warmth and the depth of relationship the Father intends

100

us to know with Him, His Son, and every other member of His forever-family.

But it takes time.

In the meanwhile, stay close together, won't you? Even if it is a little uncomfortable. One of our boys didn't, while we stood at that lookout. Although he didn't approach real danger, I did turn from watching the cloudy sunrise to see him leaning against the guardrail . . . peering over the edge . . . one full mile . . . to the bottom!

Oh, what dry-mouthed panic. My shrieked summons echoed off the canyon walls: "Get back here! And stay with us!"

It's cold. It's cloudy. And in our world today, it's a long way to the bottom. Let's stay together as a family . . . and share a few unforgettable moments.

Dear Lord . . .

I stand here dwarfed.
I cower before the projected image of what you want me to be and discover how minutely small I am by comparison.
Because of my own impurity, sinfulness,
      carnality and
         selfishness,
   I am a spiritual midget.
Surely I have grieved You, Lord.

What father would not be, at the sight of a son whose
 growth processes were seriously disturbed?

These faults which induced this dwarfing process are
 all mine, Lord.

I confess them.

You can conquer sin in the flesh;
 So with limbs shriveled and stagnated, I come
 for healing, yea, deliverance.

This monstrous self-life deserves nothing but crucifix-
ion.

So be it.

Let it be dashed to death on the Cross.

Teach me to nourish myself from the daily supply of
 the Spirit of Christ;

Let me learn to feed on Him, and thereby develop
 into the measure of the stature of His fullness.

Enlarge this shrunken heart . . .
 Quicken these leaden feet . . .
 Purge this burning conscience . . .
 Cleanse these leprous hands . . .

Wipe away the memory of so small, so petty a being
 as my own tiny self.

Build a son, Lord.

One conformed fully to the image of
 Your own dear Son,

My Savior . . .

Jesus.[6]

MAY

Power

of all Kings.

Holy Spirit, come;
  let this be Your home;
Come and dwell among all of us
  who sing this song.
Come into this place;
  shine on ev'ry face;
Fill us with Your love and grace;
Holy Spirit, come.

His Name Is Higher

Each Palm Sunday we are ushered back in time to recollect the first time a crowd rose to declare, "JESUS is the CHRIST!"

That's what the stir was about. When the people shouted, *"Hosanna to the Son of David!"* it meant one thing: This man is the King—the Messiah—the Christ! Jesus of Nazareth is the King above all.

I heard the words "Jesus Christ" uttered several times the other day, but not once were they consistent with the spirit of the Palm Sunday utterances. "GEE-zuz, KRIst!" they all said. They meant "Jesus Christ," but from blasphemous lips the name comes out as venom—frozen hatred, anger, or irritation.

We're surrounded by this violation of our Lord's glory and worthiness. It isn't simply a matter of porno literature or X-rated movies, barrooms and brothels, and foul-mouthed mechanics. Jesus is profaned in PG-rated films, in best-selling novels, by the ladylike secretary at the next desk, by the high school honor student next door.

I was tired of wincing. And yet I said nothing. It wasn't a matter of cowardice, I simply lacked conviction that words of correction would accomplish anything worthwhile. In fact, I often wonder if the blasphemer even hears himself.

Sitting in my room, alone, I struggled in prayer: *Lord, I hurt over this hateful habit that pervades my culture. I hurt for these people who mindlessly, ignorantly speak Your name in hate, anger, and frustration. Help me think, Lord. Help me understand . . . and help me love aright, as You do—in spite of the blasphemy.*

He answered me. With two deep impressions upon my soul.

The first: I suddenly saw that in a strange, reversed way, the blasphemy was a kind of self-incriminating acknowledgment of the majesty of Jesus' person. Nobody appealed to any *other* name to register their angered wish that whatever was grating them would be different. No one spoke the name of any of the founders of the world's religions. No one snarled out the name of Mohammed, Buddha, or Joseph Smith. No one cursed the name of a relative. No one indicted the government.

Why? Because the basic purpose for blasphemy is to register discontent with some frustrating fact, actually damning its presence. And if one is to do that, one must appeal to an authority who is adequate to overwhelm any fact on earth.

I know that none of those who were misusing our Lord's name were analyzing this, but the fact remains. Jesus Christ's name is spit out as an epithet a billion times a day, but the day will come when God Almighty will catch the blasphemer by the words of his or her own lips. "You appealed to My Son's authority ten thousand times in your lifetime—but not once did you acknowledge His rule in your heart."

The other impression was simply this: Since the world around is so bold to profane His name, let us be at least as bold to praise it.

He is the Lord—JESUS CHRIST!

On Casual Conversation

Recently I found myself trapped by my own self-consciousness.

Wrapped in a pleasant circle of friends, I was relishing conversation over several subjects which naturally came up. It was all rather trivial, but adequately profitable. I didn't feel I was wasting time, and I didn't feel for one moment the conversation was boring.

But I did feel something.

I felt that I needed to say something that would lead the conversation at least one rung deeper.

Mind you, it wasn't shallow talk. Nor was there anything that wasn't delightful or tasteful. Nothing to fault . . . yet I found myself letting it all stop at that.

Please let me make clear that the casual, the trivial, the merely conversational, the fun, the social—they're all fine. I am not denigrating casual conversation. But *only* that is a luxury I can't afford.

I need to make conversational investment in the kind of interaction that costs me something. Talk, like money, never bears dividends if it isn't invested. Conversations, like business, involve a risk if they are going to bear maximum profit.

In the case of this conversation, I needed to take the leap. I needed to accept the risk. I needed to indicate in some way that I wanted to talk at a little more personal level . . .

glory, honor and

... without sounding self-righteous,

... without being socially ungracious,

... without engaging in psychological catharsis,

... without coming on as a "heavyweight."

But I chickened out. Yes, I did.

I was fearful that if I suggested, "Let me tell you something that has been very much of a heart-concern to me lately," that it would jangle something of the social comfort of the situation. It wouldn't have, but I was afraid of looking dumb. I was also afraid I might get a reputation: "He always has to do something 'meaningful.'" I don't want people to think my "schtick" is turning pleasant gatherings into group therapy.

But I do want to become better acquainted with brothers and sisters in Christ than society allows.

I do want to bear burdens with people, at the points where they are really living.

And I do want to gain insights which only come when we share our hearts . . . not just our time.

Peace And Vigilance

The communist empire around the world may be crumbling, but at least one Marxist state in Asia has yet to get the message. . . .

I've just returned from a visit to Panmunjom—scene of the signing of the armistice between North and South Korea in July, 1953.

Praise Majesty

The elaborate military installation which continues there at this writing is comprised of U.N. peacekeeping forces backed by a significant contingent of U.S. troops.

A survey of the nearly forty-year history of efforts at sustaining the border against North Korean aggression is a study in the timeless and insidious persistence of evil.

No less than fifty thousand incidents of armistice violations have been documented as the South seeks to preserve its freedom from Northern intrusion. A seemingly endless web of conspiracy has been woven by the North against her fellow countrymen, ever seeking to duplicate a preposterously oppressive system below the thirty-eighth parallel. Everything from murder, bloodshed, and brutality, to armed assault and political chicanery of the worst order have been utilized.

Panmunjom is a solemn reminder that preserving peace requires vigilance. It's also a graphic picture of the need for such efforts in *all* of life.

Evil is a deadly presence orchestrated by hell in a quest to invade life at any point possible. Minds and bodies, marriages and families, businesses and finances—all are open prey to the powers of darkness. Relentlessly, intentionally, hatefully, and fiendishly, the Adversary conducts a campaign designed to depress, divide, defeat, and destroy. There are no boundaries of blessing honored by hell except those which are guarded by the vigilance of prayer, faith, and obedience to God's Word.

I've stood at the ramparts of freedom in several parts of the world. Panmunjom summarized the spirit of them all: Peace doesn't happen without being sought earnestly and preserved diligently.

So the Word of God teaches us: *Seek* peace and *pursue* it; blessed are the *peacemakers*; let the peace of God *rule* in your hearts (1 Peter 3:11, Matthew 5:9, Colossians

3:15). To keep our hearts and minds under the protection and power of God's peace, we are told to fix our minds against a takeover by either anxiety or impurity (Philippians 4:6-8).

In short—whatever it is . . . yourself, your mind, your body, your family, your job, your life—peace must be *preserved*.

He will keep in perfect peace all whose minds are stayed on Him (Isaiah 26:3). Set yourself in partnership with Him. The Prince of Peace is able to sustain peace in your life and mind, even in the face of the Enemy's endlessly evil efforts.

The power is God's, but the vigilance is ours.

The Power of Song

Can we even begin to understand the power of song?

By "song" I mean more than mouthing words to a line of music. I am referring to the burst of melody that accompanies the announcement of words which, with understanding, are declared in praise to God.

Scripture describes a group in David's time who were "under the direction of their father for song" and who were "instructed in the songs of the LORD" (1 Chronicles 25:6,7). What a dramatic parallel might be found in today's church, if we would allow ourselves to come under the directing hand of the Father . . . if we would allow His Spirit to teach us the essence of the power of song.

flow from His

Consider God's Word on this:

"Sing, O barren,
You who have not borne!
Break forth into singing, and cry aloud,
You who have not travailed with child!
For more are the children of the desolate
Than the children of the married woman," says the
*   Lord (Isaiah 54:1).*

This passage tells us to sing when barrenness has locked out fruitfulness. It clearly intimates that the power of song creates a setting in which life may be conceived and brought to full delivery.

For this cause everyone who is godly shall pray to You
In a time when You may be found;
Surely in a flood of great waters
They shall not come near him.
You are my hiding place;
You shall preserve me from trouble;
You shall surround me with songs of deliverance
*   (Psalm 32:6,7).*

David instructs us of the power of song to deliver from bondage. Oppressive works of hell cannot tolerate the singing of saints who refuse to be quenched in their spirit when bondage threatens. They sing instead!

And they rose early in the morning and went out into the Wilderness of Tekoa; and as they went out, Jehoshaphat stood and said, "Hear me, O Judah and you inhabitants of Jerusalem: Believe in the Lord your God, and you shall be established; believe His prophets, and you shall prosper."

And when he had consulted with the people, he appointed those who should sing to the Lord, and who should praise the beauty of holiness, as they went out before the army and were saying:

"Praise the LORD,
For His mercy endures forever"
(2 Chronicles 20:20,21).

King Jehoshaphat's people demonstrate the sheer power of praise in this classic Old Testament story of Judah marching to battle with the choir leading her troops. The message: If the battle is the Lord's, then enter it praising Him—it scatters the opposition every time.

Let the word of Christ dwell in you richly in all wisdom, teaching and admonishing one another in psalms and hymns and spiritual songs, singing with grace in your hearts to the Lord (Colossians 3:16).

And do not be drunk with wine, in which is dissipation; but be filled with the Spirit, speaking to one another in psalms and hymns and spiritual songs, singing and making melody in your heart to the Lord (Ephesians 5:18,19).

Paul's words from two letters blend together to teach us the power of song to (1) keep you filled with the Holy Spirit, and (2) make the Word of God rich in its action within your soul and spirit. It seems that "song" may provide the spiritual enzymes by which the "meat of the Word" is broken down within us and assimilated into our lives.

Where were you when I laid the foundations of the earth?
Tell Me, if you have understanding.
Who determined its measurements?
Surely you know!
Or who stretched the line upon it?
To what were its foundations fastened?
Or who laid its cornerstone,
When the morning stars sang together,
And all the sons of God shouted for joy?
(Job 38:4-7).

Job's encounter with God produced these ancient words. The setting is "the beginning," at creation; and the scene notes how God's majestic act of bringing our world into being was accompanied by angelic song.

I wonder about that.

I wonder if the Lord might not want us to understand that if we would sing more, it might release Him to work far more creatively in our life circumstances. Frankly, I think so.

So it's no small wonder Paul says, "I will sing with the spirit, and I will also sing with the understanding" (1 Corinthians 14:15). He knows what he is talking about. Acts 16:25-34 records something of his experience with song—shattering the bondage of a Philippian dungeon and introducing salvation to a household. Thus he learned: We are not called to sing merely with gusto—but with Holy Spirit-begotten understanding and energy.

That kind of song shattered chains and broke open prison doors for Paul. Think what it might do for you.

Who's Afraid? Me.

Remember the song the three little piggies sang in the cartoon? "Who's afraid of the big bad wolf?" Their jolly bravado was radically changed when actual confrontation came. But, of course, after their adversary was boiled in the pot, trying to climb down Practical Pig's chimney, they struck up the song again.

I suppose there are better texts from which to teach on overcoming fear, but that episode came so clearly to mind I couldn't resist running it through the memory mill. The story does emphasize two critical points:

1. *It's easy to be fearless until fear comes upon you.*

That observation also has a flip side: To be afraid is not the same thing as being *overcome* by fear. Some view a life of faith as one that never fears. Wrong! Listen to Paul, for example: "Within were fears," he says, describing his own trials (2 Corinthians 7:5, KJV).

To listen to some proponents of the believing life, you would think that every encounter with difficulty should be met with a smile, a shrug, a scripture, and a "Who's afraid?"

I have confronted circumstances—both real and imagined—and have been shot through with terror or unnerved with sorrow, depending upon the situation. You probably have, too. Don't let anyone tell you he or she always skips and dances in the face of fear. And don't—I repeat—*don't* feel guilty because you *do* experience fear.

But . . .

2. *What counts is what you DO with fear.*

As with the piggies, fear may dampen your song, chase you, and bring squeals of panic. So run. Don't be ashamed. Run. But run in the right direction: "The name of the LORD is a strong tower; The righteous run to it and are safe" (Proverbs 18:10).

Once inside the safety of Jesus' authoritative name, *force fear into your mold.* Remember Practical Pig? For the wolf to get in that pig's "strong tower," he had to come down the chimney.

Light the fires of faith with prayer: "Don't keep on worrying about anything, but in everything pray! Then God's peace will guard you like a sentinel—your heart and mind secured" (Philippians 4:6, paraphrase). Our adversary can't make it by that blazing wall of protection.

> *. . . Fan into flame the gift of God, which is in you through the laying on of my hands. For God did not give us a spirit of timidity, but a spirit of power, of love and of self-discipline (2 Timothy 1:6-7, NIV).*

Reignite the fire of the Holy Spirit. Meet fear with flame.

As Jesus' sheep, we're certainly not pigs . . . but we still have a wolf to deal with. When he howls, c'mon inside the Refuge. And turn on the burners!

How Do You Draw Closer to Jesus?

I was talking the other day to a successful business-man whose nephew began attending our church a couple of years ago. Although the businessman is a fruitful Christian attending a Bible-believing church, he was impressed with something he saw in his relative.

"Something about his church has really led to strong growth in his life," he said. "Something about the way you urge people to be honest, childlike, and open with God—and with one another."

He went on to elaborate how much that nephew has ministered to him over the past few months. If it weren't that I know this man to be a man of integrity, I would think he was simply attempting to flatter. But he wasn't. He was merely relating what I must honestly say is a kind of thing I've heard time and again. I don't hesitate to say that, because I know full well it is nothing to my credit.

What he was noticing in that relative of his is precisely what Jesus came to work in all of us. Whenever you begin to open up to the real Jesus in a real way through the Word and by the Spirit, things happen. I'm persuaded there are a combination of things basic to this occurring in a person's life, and when the man I mentioned asked me how I thought this happened in people, I enumerated these things:

1. *Become open and forthright in worship.* Biblical worship is humbling. It strikes at the heart of cultural resistance, human pride, and religious formalism. Simple, open praise and worship softens the heart and prepares us for transformation.

2. *Be filled with the Holy Spirit.* The New Testament reveals this experience to be more than merely an entry into the resource of God's power. It also involves making ourselves vulnerable to the Holy Spirit's transcending our own intellect with His control. He doesn't make robots or produce trances, but He does show us God isn't as impressed with our brains as we tend to be.

3. *Become involved in transparent fellowship.* Small groups and interactive relationships are the Lord's tools for keeping us honestly in touch with others . . . and with ourselves. There is nothing more shaping than submitting yourselves to the mutually loving and confrontive kind of relationship that New Testament integrity calls for and makes possible. "Walking in the light, we have fellowship with one another" (1 John 1:7, paraphrase).

How do we draw closer to Jesus? I think it costs us more than acquiring information or performing religious tasks. It cuts to the quick of our character—

—facing us up to God in worship,

—opening us up to the Holy Spirit in simplicity and worship, and

—drawing us together with God's people.

Magnify, come,

I Believe In the Holy Spirit

I believe in the Holy Spirit, revealed in Scripture as personal and knowable; one in being with the Father and the Son, and with them almighty, all-knowing, and ever-present.

Because I believe this, I will worship and welcome Him in all aspects and affairs of my life. His almightiness has been promised to instruct and teach me, and His constant presence has been promised to glorify the Lord Jesus in me and to bear witness to the Lord Jesus through me.

I believe in the Holy Spirit of love, who baptizes believers into the Body of Christ and through whose presence God's love is poured forth into our hearts. It is His convincing work that brings men to Christ, His regenerating work that produces new life within, His indwelling that produces fruitfulness, and His guiding that directs obedience to the Father's Word.

Because I believe this, I entertain the Holy Spirit's presence in my heart. As I began in the Spirit, so shall I walk in newness of life by His working in me. I will respect and respond to Him as He continually teaches me to turn from sin, as He promotes true holiness within me, and as He develops His promised fruit in my character.

I believe in the Holy Spirit of power, by whom the Father anointed Jesus' ministry, and with whom Jesus Himself baptizes all who will receive His enduement of ability. By this empowering, the works which Christ did, we may do also, with expectation of even greater things through the gifts the Holy Spirit distributes through us who believe in the Lord Jesus.

Because I believe this, I openly acknowledge my desire and express my request that Christ my Lord overflow my life with the promised Spirit from on high. Without presumption, I believe that I shall see the manifest fullness of Jesus' love and power demonstrated through my life. I believe I will receive daily evidence of His grace and regular evidence of Christ's miracle life as I employ the gifts the Holy Spirit affords.

With the Spirit of these *truths* graciously available to me, I will bow in humble submission to His authority, grow in tender sensitivity to His love, and offer myself in surrender to the workings of His power.

Supporting Scriptures:

Matthew 28:19; 2 Corinthians 13:14; 1 John 5:7; Acts 13:2; Psalm 139:7-12; Zechariah 4:6; Joel 2:28; Acts 1:8, 2:38-39; John 15:26, 16:7-14.

1 Corinthians 12:12-13; Romans 5:5; John 3:8; Galatians 5:22-25; Ephesians 4:30-32; 2 Corinthians 3:17-18; Galatians 3:3.

Acts 10:38; Luke 24:49; Romans 8:1-17; John 1:33; Ephesians 3:16-19; 1 Corinthians 12:7-11.

Some Things We Dare Not Forget

Beloved, I now write to you this second epistle (in both of which I stir up your pure minds by way of reminder), that you may be mindful of the words which were spoken before by the holy prophets, and of the commandment of us the apostles of the Lord and Savior (2 Peter 3:1-2).

the King Maje

Beloved, while I was very diligent to write to you concerning our common salvation, I found it necessary to write to you exhorting you to contend earnestly for the faith which was once for all delivered to the saints (Jude 3).

Truth stands on its own, but in our hearts and minds its application needs the buttressing effect of "remindings."

If you groan, as I do, over the steep moral decline of our nation, let the words on this page summon you to a rededication of yourself to prayer, fasting, and intercession.

As God's people, there are some things we dare not forget.

Only prayer can bring kingdom power.

Jesus' instruction in Luke 11:1-4 and Matthew 6:9-13 is clear. The love and power of the Father's will and rule can only be known earth-side if the redeemed will call out for it. Prayer is no gamble. It is no bingo match or waiting to see if you get the door prize. Prayer works. "Ask and you will receive" (Luke 11:9, paraphrase). We aren't to substitute prayer for action, but activity will never substitute for prayer. He who prays without working is in ignorance; but he who works without praying is a fool.

Only fasting can break some hellish bondage.

The episode of the child's deliverance recorded in Matthew 17:14-21 is poignant and pointed. It is poignant because a boy is set free from the torment of demonic power; it is pointed as Jesus underscores the irreplaceable key to that liberation: prayer and fasting (v. 21).

Fasting is not a crowbar wedging God into action. It is not a mark of peculiar holiness—but it leaves its mark on peculiarly hellish situations. While there is no substitute for the power of the blood of the Cross in freeing mankind, fasting is an instrument that can break barricades to the application of that power.

Only intercession can guarantee good government.

First Timothy 2:1-4 not only commands believers to intercede for those who hold governmental leadership, but it describes a society of peace and quiet which can result. I am often asked my feelings about certain candidates during election years. I'll tell you my response: I pray for them all! One of them is God's man or woman for the job of strengthening this land in righteousness. I don't discourage political involvement—not at all. But let every believer intercede.

Together, let us roll back the encroaching darkness and extend the light and glory of Christ upon the face of our nation. Intercession, energized by the Holy Spirit, is the key (James 5:16-18).

Behold The Living God

Behold the living God
who moves among us now.
The Lord of all creation comes
with one eternal vow.
To those who humbly seek Him,
who deep contrition feel,
By His own loving power
He will Himself reveal.
Behold the Word of God,
declared in Spirit power;
Ignited by the Holy Ghost,
its pages glow this hour.
Lord, penetrate our hearts;
now Thy Holy Sword unsheath.
Cut through our bent to sinning,
destroy our unbelief.

Behold the living Christ,
His presence now we feel.
O loving Lord, be now adored,
as reverently we kneel.
Speak peace and full forgiveness,
establish full control.
Extend Thy hand in healing;
all broken lives make whole.

Behold the living God,
His majesty confess,
His holiness extol in awe,
declare His changelessness.
With open hearts we worship,
with upraised hands we praise.
Our voices laud in concert,
Thou Lord, Ancient of Days.

Refrain:

Blessed Holy Spirit, move among us now—
Show to us Thy Presence, Thy best gifts endow.
Exalt the name of Jesus, anoint the Word proclaimed.
Transform, refill, consume us with sacred tongues of flame.[7]

JUNE

Triumph

of all Kings.

Come and be King, come even now,
Come now and rule by Your grace.
Lord Jesus, come and be King.

Taking It By Force

From the days of John the Baptist until now the king-dom of heaven suffers violence, and the violent take it by force (Matthew 11:12).

These are among Christ's least understood words. They follow on the heels of His words about John the Baptist's break from the traditional image of a "religious person." He says, in effect, "If you went out to see Mr. Cool-and-Sophisticated, he had to be a disappointment!"

There's something blunt, rough, and unpolished about Kingdom people. Yet we're called to be gentle, harmless, gracious, and hospitable, too. How do those traits merge?

I believe the answer is in our *spirit*—the way we approach spiritual things. A Kingdom person is never called to reduce his or her sensitivity toward people, tenderness in loving, or generosity of attitude. To the contrary, you can count on a genuine believer to mature into a lovely lady or a real gentleman.

But when you get that lady or gentleman face-to-face with a spiritual challenge, she or he will become violent. The person will become indignant with the gall of the devil to attempt to encroach upon a realm wherein Christ has worked redemption. Such believers are impatient with demons and antagonistic toward any of hell's working. A person who has begun to understand the nature of the spiritual struggle will be kind in demeanor toward people, but vicious in his or her prayer life and spiritual warfare.

We don't need "mild-mannered Clark Kent" saints when super-prayer is the order of the day. There are times to get down on the prayer-bones, call out with strong cryings, seek hard after God, and strike down the work of the devil.

I don't know how to precisely describe this to you, but I know how it works in me. Quite often, I find myself drifting in a kind of prayer limbo. Sort of "asking" God to "help" with some problem. Then, feeling I'm getting nowhere, I am jerked to the awareness that I'm praying the wrong way.

I'm begging when I ought to be battling.

I need to rise up in violent, fervent prayer to "possess the land" under discussion. It's as though the Father is saying, "You've taken counsel with Me long enough. YOU go forth against the enemy—and I'll go before you."

Please understand. This violence is not a shrieking wrestling match to attempt to twist something from God's hand which He only reluctantly wants us to have.

No.

But it *is* a contest. There is a "contending" that is needed, and the Holy Spirit wants to bring us all to a place of understanding that some obstacles yield before us only by forcible praying.

This is difficult to describe without sounding as though the accomplishment is a mere effort of human energy and emotionalism. It is neither. It is rather a release of divine intervention proportionate to our willingness to execute God's will in authoritative praying.

Read Psalm 149 . . . it's all there.

Begin with worship and praise.

Sing to the LORD a new song,
And His praise in the congregation of saints.

Let Israel rejoice in their Maker;
Let the children of Zion be joyful in their King.
Let them praise His name with the dance (vv. 1-3).

Acknowledge your place in Christ—"humble" under His authoritative Lordship, and securely confident in His salvation, His finished work at Calvary.

For the LORD takes pleasure in His people;
He will beautify the humble with salvation.

Let the saints be joyful in glory;
Let them sing aloud on their beds (vv. 4-5).

Then attack! Take the enemy off guard, and possess the land—the victory you seek—by force.

Let the high praises of God be in their mouth,
And a two-edged sword in their hand,
To execute vengeance on the nations,
And punishments on the peoples;
To bind their kings with chains,
And their nobles with fetters of iron;
To execute on them the written judgment
(vv. 6-9a).

As the psalmist says, "This honor have all His saints. Praise the LORD!" (v. 9b).

glory, honor and

I Believe In The Second Coming of Jesus Christ

I believe in the second coming of Jesus Christ. I believe that He who literally and physically ascended from the Mount of Olives forty days after His resurrection, shall come again in like manner, personally returning to this earth according to the prophets and His promise.

Because I believe this, I can live unconfused within the chaos of our society's decline. I can live sustained beyond whatever stress or trial I may face, for I have a view of the future that gives a point to human history and an anticipated triumph beyond all tribulation.

I believe His return is imminent. It is unpredictable and immediately possible at any moment. I believe this has been the stance of the Church from the earliest day until now, and that expectancy is to be constant and undiminished until the trumpet sounds and He descends from heaven with a shout.

Because I believe this, I reject any system of human reason or dogma which preempts anticipating His returning TODAY, or which attempts to excite interest by predicting a day or date of His coming. My expectancy does not require the fuel of humanly devised systems of prophecy, however scriptural their pretense, for my heart is nourished by His own words alone: "Behold, I come quickly."

I believe He is coming for His Church, as a Bridegroom seeking a bride of virginal purity and unswerving devotion. I believe that His commitment to His Church is complete; until He comes we may rest in His promise never to forsake us, to nourish and keep us, and to bring the obedient along a path of growth and holiness so as to assure our readiness to meet Him at His coming.

Because I believe this, I choose to live each day and govern my activities as a wise servant who expects His Master's return, and not as one who presumes that his Lord is delaying His coming. I will to walk with Him in constant fellowship, purify myself even as He is pure, and live as one whose heart daily utters the prayer, "Even so, come Lord Jesus."

I believe at His coming all His Church shall be caught up into His presence, shall join Him in His judging the earth as He establishes His righteous Kingdom upon the whole earth, and that our decision in this present age determines who those shall be that will reign with Him as priests and kings unto our God.

Because I believe this, I serve Him now as one engaged faithfully in His Kingdom enterprises, doing the business of the Master in reaching to the lost, teaching the unlearned, and extending His life and love by every means; knowing that the night is coming when no more work shall be allowed, and that the dawn of the ultimate day will bring a final accounting at His coming.

With such a hope as this, I am moved to live expectantly, walk purely, and serve faithfully, in the assurance that He who has prepared a place for me is coming again to receive me to Himself.

Supporting Scriptures:

Acts 1:9-11; Daniel 2:44, 7:9,10; John 14:1-3; Revelation 21:1-7.

Mark 13:32; Revelation 22:7; 1 Thessalonians 4:16; 1 Corinthians 15:51,52; Matthew 24:24-27; 2 Peter 3:1-13.

Matthew 25:1-13; Ephesians 5:25-27; Matthew 28:20; Luke 12:42-48; 2 Corinthians 11:2; 1 John 3:2,3; Revelation 22:20; 1 Corinthians 16:22.

1 Thessalonians 4:17; Matthew 24:21-31, 13:24-30, 37-43; Revelation 5:10; Matthew 24:14; Luke 19:13; Mark 16:15-20; John 9:4,5; Matthew 16:26,27; 1 Thessalonians 5:1-10; Philippians 1:6.

The Story of Two Days

I was lower than a cockroach in the second sub-basement.

The convergence of a combination of factors was bringing me down. *Way down*. I seemed completely unable to sift through the mountainous sense of foreboding overshadowing me.

Condemnation was settling in.

To begin with, I was mindful of my own unfulfilled commitments. *You said you would write. You were going to give more time to prayer. You can't trust God now, because you've not been faithful to all the things you know you ought to be doing.*

A voice—I was sure it was my own—kept chanting to me. *The problem is you. The problem is you. The problem is you.*

I would find verses—not in my regular reading, but words that seemed to jump out of the woodwork at me and snag my mind. *God has lost patience with you*, they seemed to say. *You're in danger of incurring His judgment. You are on the brink of something horrible.*

I was near despair. Growing inwardly irritable and short. Feeling that even *that* was further evidence of my miserableness.

I virtually crawled to a place of prayer. My words were feeble in tone, honest in confession, simple in request, inquiring of the Lord.

You know my heart, Father! I don't want to do anything

flow from His

other than Your will. Where my flesh fails, I have no hope out-side your patience and forgiveness. Where my soul quails in the face of the winds of adversity, where my mind crunches under the pressure of condemnation or conviction—I don't know which if You don't support me, I can't bear it. Father, help me. I'm tired. Lift me . . . lead me.

The words came haltingly, and the prayer trailed off to an inconclusive conclusion with my semi-whispering of "in Jesus' name," sounding anything but faith-like or inspiring.

Nothing happened for about two hours. (There have been times in the past when nothing happened for two weeks!) And then a letter crossed my desk . . . and within another hour two people came into my office. What the letter said and what the people did are entire stories in themselves, but the point is—the Father reached to me!

He lifted me. He silenced the Accuser. He quenched doubt. He smothered condemnation. He resurrected my soul from its burial beneath circumstances. He shed light on His way for me. He confirmed my sonship, conferred His blessings, and delivered me from oppression.

That's the story of my past two days. Thursday and Friday. And that's my counsel to you if you've been set-ting up housekeeping in the basement. If you can't run, walk to a place of prayer. If you can't walk, *crawl*.

It doesn't matter how you get there, what counts is Whom you'll meet there.

An Epitaph

Luanne, my sister, went home last Sunday.

Jesus met her at 11:30 in the morning, while I was preaching the third service on "The God Who Works in the Dark."

Beside her bed, just a few blocks from my pulpit, my father and mother had bowed a few hours before.

Father, she's Yours. We release her into Your strong hands, in Jesus' name.

We had all fought a good fight. No enemy, not even cancer, and no specter, not even death, could drive out the confident sense of rejoicing: "All is well! Through Christ our Conqueror, all is well!"

A dozen stories long to be told, for as I moved through the ensuing hours I witnessed and experienced one miracle of God's grace after another. Oh! The marvel of God's ways . . . unsearchable . . . past finding out . . . *until you're there by His leading.* And then you discover wisdom, peace, grace, joy, power, and wonder you've never known before.

I sat with Duane, my brother-in-law, in the mortuary on Monday morning . . . helping him with decisions . . . praying for guidance on simple and large matters . . . watching it all flow together . . . and then . . .

"Jack, would you write the wording for the tablet that will mark Luanne's grave?"

My pencil scrawled out some thoughts. Words didn't seem enough. There were too few of them to empty my heart. I finalized a statement and prepared to read it to Duane and my father, seated across the room.

First, her name, birthdate, and homegoing date, and then: "Duane's faithful wife, Amy and David's loving mother. She worshiped the Living God. She glorified His Son Jesus. And she gave herself to win China for Christ."

Then I stopped. "No. Wait." My pencil scratched a hasty edit, converting the past tense into the present: "She *worships* the Living God, and she *glorifies* Jesus Christ. . . . "

Ah, praise God! To write an epitaph for a graduated saint, you need to watch your tenses. She's still worshiping. Oh, how she's worshiping Him!

So am I.

That's not exactly the way 1 John 4:18 reads in the old King James. The word there is, "Fear hath *torment*." Nevertheless, fear does take potshots at each of us. Without realizing it, we begin ducking and dodging.

Recognizing a clear-cut, head-on attack of a massive spirit of fear can be a challenge. We become afraid to be bold, tearing ourselves up with self-scrutiny, always inclined to function from a defensive stance rather than from the solidity of a positive-in-faith position.

One shot is aimed at filling our minds with self-doubt, suggestions that we never do anything right. I don't mean anyone actually *says* that . . . anyone *visible*, I mean. But just as Jesus countered temptation with the Word, so can we. Scripture says that we have the mind of Christ and that He is directing our paths (1 Corinthians 2:16, Proverbs 3:6).

Another shot is physical sickness as a specific result of a subtle and calculated work of fear.

Our Adversary is doing everything possible to sink us. The waters we're navigating seem to be boiling with warheads, a tormenting presence of perpetual distraction.

Then Jesus points out the real problem: We *defend against* attack rather than *going on* the attack. "No weapon formed against you shall prosper," His voice rings out (Isaiah 54:17).

You remember the words of Admiral Farragut at the battle of Mobile Bay. When surrounded by attackers, *he chose the course of bold action rather than cautious defense.* His words speak out across the years, "Damn the torpedoes! Full speed ahead!"

That may not be a very pastoral thing to say . . . but when you face this kind of thing, let me encourage you to get your hand back on the throttle. Don't let Satan even slow you down long enough to dodge his hell-shots. Make your speech: Send them back with that word, and "full speed ahead."

In the Name of Him who knows what to do with torpedoes,

Amen!

There's a Bright Golden Haze on the Meadow

The peaceful setting of Rodgers and Hammerstein's great musical *Oklahoma!* comes to mind this morning. I feel absolutely euphoric with a sense of marvelous confidence concerning God's dealings in my life, home, and church. Having just returned from Japan, one might more expect me to be singing excerpts from *Madame Butterfly* . . . but "O What a Beautiful Morning" is on my lips instead.

Now, understand, I'm not without pressures trying my faith. I'm not without the personal sense of current "growing pains," which any healthy believer experiences sporadically. To the contrary, and quite frankly, I'm right on the edge of one of the greatest challenges of my life.

But it's a good day.

It's a good day because I'm in touch with Jesus.

Personal touch. Simple touch. Not see-and-feel touch, but genuine walk-talk-and-trust touch.

I am becoming more and more impressed with the summons to simplicity that Jesus issues: "Follow Me . . . trust Me . . . learn of Me. . . ." He makes no grand promises of a rose-strewn pathway. He doesn't roll out a blueprint of predictable details forecasting our tomorrows, nor does He guarantee that we will ever arrive at some comfortable state of perfected accomplishment. Rather, He says, "In the world you will have tribulation." He asserts, "Satan will desire to sift you as wheat," and He disciples with the commission, "Take up My cross."

He's constantly stretching me. You too?

Of course. You too. And it's enough to make you sometimes wonder what kind of a bargain you got when you gave over to this Man. He is so convinced of His capacity to make us people of large purpose, genuine significance, and high destiny that He keeps on leading us forward.

E. M. Bounds had words for it when he often used the expression, "We must always be on the stretch for God." It's not a rack of torture, but it certainly is a path of growth.

But best of all, He's always there. That's what makes any season of trial, any call to faith, any burden of responsibility a glory-time. Jesus is there. Not a doctrine about Him. Not an idea of what He's like. Not a memory of some past experience.

No. Just Him. Jesus, my living Lord—here in the present tense.

So in whatever I face, there's rejoicing.

In whatever the "stretch," there's resiliency.

In whatever the demand there are resources. Because He is here. Right now. It's the simplest and the most profound truth I know: "Lo, I am with you always."

When this sheep named Jack is accompanied by his Great Shepherd named Jesus, the whole meadow lights up. Tried? Yes. Stretched? Yes. Problemed? Yes. But Jesus is here, and because of that, "I've got a beautiful feeling—everything's going my way."

The Sum of a Summer

Approaching the mellow weeks of summer, whether conscious of it or not, we all make a choice concerning the investment of our time.

Most of us are programmed to choose "slackening of pace" as normative for the ensuing months, until Labor Day announces the end to the surrealism that summer tends to become. Any optional choice must be made against the grain of established habit. That choice?

To choose growth.

In the natural order of things—crops, trees, flowers—everything grows dramatically during summer time. Notably absent from that process is heavy demand—it's simply the creative order of development. In other words, God's program of summer time growth isn't *sweaty*, it just happens. Beautifully. Abundantly. But only when things are in alignment with His order.

Flowers, for example, must be in the right environment to receive water and nutrients. Too much shade, not enough water, neglect of weeding—these factors must be guarded against and *then* growth is natural, easy, and beautiful.

In the spiritual order of things, I believe it's much the same. I *don't* believe God wants our summer to be less than fulfilling and refreshing in its variety of experiences. But I *do* believe He wants us all to grow up and go forward, not accepting the slothful mode of passive, slack-to-duty attitude a usual summertime mentality can engender.

We've all heard and hummed Gershwin's "Summertime": *Summertime . . . and the livin' is easy*. The laid-back, lackadaisical drawl of the song's lyric and music form slides you down in your hammock, plunks a lemonade in your hand, and hypnotizes you. It seems to induce a semi-comatose state, oozing with syrupy indifference, and lamely grinning from a face dewy with humidity.

Wake up, saints! I don't want to take away summer's fun, festivity, or recreation, but I do want to issue a call against spiritual drowsiness. Let's move ahead in Christ with three full months of *living*, as opposed to ninety days of resignation to passivity.

Start TODAY. Pointedly pursue a productive season. Can't think of how to get started? Here are a few suggestions:

1. *Pick out at least two books to read.*

I've selected five already, which span the distance from Bible doctrine and current theological issues to a biography of one of history's greatest political leaders. Plan on growing through reading.

2. *Share your life in a special way.*

Plan on and pray toward at least one distinct occasion where you will invite a person you know who is not yet a believer to a pleasant, enjoyable occasion of recreation or dining. A picnic, golf game, a trip to the beach or the lake, a barbecue on your patio . . . the list goes on. Don't try and "blow 'em away with hot gospel." Simply show friendship, and let the life and love of Jesus Christ be manifest in your home, your demeanor, and, to whatever degree the door opens, with your words.

3. *Make a fresh commitment to "the basics."*

Pray, read, and memorize. Get the growth basics down pat, and don't let up even when you're on vacation.

4. *Seek the Holy Spirit's plan for your summer.*

He has one, you know. Look for the thread of His plan for you through the maze of sunny days. With the growth, He has something glorious as well; something specifically custom-made for you and your personal fruitfulness. I'm praying you'll discover that "something" as we move through June, July, and August.

By means of the Spirit's leading, I believe we can all come to the end of the season and say, "The sum of my summer was *growth*.

When Man Won't Let Go

That night Jacob got up . . . and crossed the ford of the Jabbok. . . . So Jacob was left alone, and a man wrestled with him till daybreak. When the man saw that he could not overpower him, he touched the socket of Jacob's hip so that his hip was wrenched as he wrestled with the man. Then the man said, "Let me go, for it is daybreak."

But Jacob replied, "I will not let you go unless you bless me."

The man asked him, "What is your name?"

"Jacob," he answered.

Then the man said, "Your name will no longer be Jacob, but Israel, because you have struggled with God and with men and have overcome."

. . . So Jacob called the place Peniel, saying, "It is because I saw God face to face, and yet my life was spared" (Genesis 32:22, 24-28, 30, NIV).

Jacob wrestled with a heavenly opponent all night long and was commended and rewarded as daylight broke over the Jabbok.

His reward: the gift of a new identity. "Your name will no longer be Jacob, but Israel"(vs. 28).

To the understanding heart, the statement is pregnant with significance. It demonstrates the readiness of God to grant new identity and new dimensions of responsibility to those who refuse to give up (*Israel* means "he struggles with God").

This is not to suggest an earned reward, as though God only relents to those who wrestle Him to the ground and force gifts from His hand. But it does indicate a truth which balances the great principles of grace and giving from God's hand. God is looking for those who will move into partnership with Him in the struggle for mankind. He is searching for those who will grow up, who will lay hold of prayer responsibility, who will accept fundamental disciplines of the Jesus-life, who will give unselfishly, who will speak openly.

In short, God rejoices in people who "hang in there" because they know it will make a difference in their world.

True, persistence and diligence have nothing to do with our salvation. "White-knuckled religion" is totally removed from the reality of the Good News in Christ. We are accepted and beloved in Him wholly apart from our own works. You don't get more saved by trying harder, and no "We Tried Harder" badges will appear in heaven. The sheer magnanimity of God's grace and giving toward us explodes any ideology that suggests any deeds of yours or mine will improve anything about our position or acceptance with the eternal Father.

BUT. Big word. BUT—the party's not over with the celebration of our protected and secured standing before Him. His desire is not only that we learn to *receive* His love, it is also that we learn to *release* His love. That's where discipline, faithfulness, service, witness, giving, intercession, and general "persistence in things spiritual" come in.

The pathway to heaven is paved with gold, purchased in full through the Cross, and freely traversed by all who will come to God through Jesus Christ. But the pathways to the world—paths He prods us toward as ministers of His life, His power, His love and mercy—are rocky, thorn-strewn, and uphill all the way.

You eventually come to the place where you must make a decision: Will I simply take heaven as God's gift and receive His love solely as an individual . . . or will I take and receive all He offers and then—*and then*—give myself back for His use and His purposes?

A "yes" to the first question will not make you less loved, nor will a "yes" to the second question improve your status before God.

But a "yes" on number two will bring a reward. It is the dimension of fellowship with Christ the Lord that is known only to those who learn the *real* meaning of "bearing His cross."

If that latter path tugs at your heart today, let me ask you to do two things: (1) PLEDGE YOURSELF to new levels of commitment in fasting, prayer, and intercession; (2) MINISTER. Where you are . . . now. Reach. Touch. Love. Take hold of God and refuse to let go. Let's fulfill the destiny He redeemed us to know.

Great Deliverance—Mighty Redemption

Once in all hist'ry,
O great the myst'ry
        God came to earth veiled in flesh
        so man could see.
In Christ the Savior,
God showed His favor
        He to redeem us
        ascended Calvary.

Chorus:

        Great deliverance!
        Mighty redemption!
                That can reach the lost like me,
                Cleanse from guilt and set me free.
        So I'll shout, "Hallelujah!"
        And, "Praise God Jehovah!"
                For that great deliverance and great victory.

        Dark was the hour,
        Hell-born the power
                Which tore the flesh of the Lamb
                spent on the Tree.
        Death now partaking—
        Hell's power breaking—
                Hear "It is finished!"
                The Lamb cries, "Victory!"

Repeat Chorus

Come to the Mountain—
Bathe in the Fountain
        Wash in the blood Jesus shed
        upon that Cross.
Call Jesus' Name now—
Come make your claim now,
        He'll break your bondage;
        redeem your every loss.

Repeat Chorus[8]

JULY

Praise

p His Majesty

Join your hand with mine,
Let our faith combine
For in prayer -
There is nothing impossible.

The First Alternative

Humankind waits until all else fails. Then we pray.

Disciples of Jesus are prayer-learners: We learn to pray in prayer and by prayer. Like everything else with discipleship, there is a constant growth pattern available to us. Nothing happens fast, but the joy we experience is just in knowing *something is happening*.

Where are you, right now, in prayer-learning?

It's a highly important question. Important to you, personally, and important to the body of Christ, collectively. In my own life, as Christ's man, wanting to learn His lifestyle with the Holy Spirit's help, I have found some challenging passages inviting my response to more prayer.

I see Jesus at prayer, and it moves me:

. . . He withdrew to be alone in prayer
(Mark 6:46; Luke 9:18, 22:41);

. . . He prayed for extended periods of time
(Mark 1:35, Luke 6:12);

. . . He prayed frequently
(Luke 5:15,16).

I hear Jesus teaching prayer, and it prompts me to action:

glory, honor, and

. . . He taught solitude in prayer
(Matthew 6:6);

. . . He taught humility and tenacity in prayer
(Luke 11:1-13);

. . . He taught faithfulness in prayer
(Luke 18:1);

. . . He taught power in prayer
(Mark 11:22-26).

Why do we get so busy at everything other than prayer? Why do we say so often, "Well, I've prayed, but what can I *do*?" Why does our flesh find it so painfully necessary to "sweat it," rather than to "cast" it? (Psalm 55:22, 1 Peter 5:7). Why don't messages like those in the hymns "What a Friend We Have in Jesus" and "Take Your Burden to the Lord and Leave It There" lay permanent hold on our soul? What can you and I do today—right now—that will begin to make a difference in this all-important area of our lives?

Answer:

Begin to pray and praise immediately when different situations arise. Start now.

Speak to Jesus about each matter that begins to trouble you. Don't wait.

Cease from the exhausting toil of carrying worries and cares on your own shoulders. Release them.

Seize every opportunity to pray with and for people. Take advantage.

Let me suggest some possibilities for additional action: (1) This week, don't get into bed without first getting beside it. Review the day, and leave all unresolved matters with Him. (2) This week, go to a prayer meeting or pray with one or two other Christian friends. The sharing in prayer will be a strength to you and to those you pray for. (3) This month, set aside half a day (say, from 8:00 to 11:00 or noon on a day off, or take an evening) and get alone with the Savior—in the Word and prayer.

You may be surprised to see yourself become a person of power in prayer . . . a person who comes to learn that when you have prayed, you have done the most completely adequate thing that can be done.

When you've done that, "anything else" will be taken care of by Him who "does all things well."

Behind The Guardrail

One minute last Monday my car was in the flow of five o'clock traffic. The next, it was bouncing clumsily toward the side of the freeway, my tire blown and pulpy, the rim grinding on the pavement.

My mind was racing in a dozen directions: *I have to get to the church—the dinner begins in just over an hour . . . Have to get the details finalized . . . The traffic is so fast . . . I've never stopped on the freeway . . . Scary . . . How do those who work here get used to it? . . . The wind is blowing so hard . . . Gusts from passing trucks on top of it . . . Roadside uneven here . . . Do I dare jack the car up? . . . Will it tip over? . . . Nearly a mile to off-ramp . . . Should I risk wrecking something and drive it . . . Better walk to the call box . . . How do they work, anyway? . . . Who gets called? . . . This is wild . . . Can't believe it . . . A new tire, too!*

The whirl of thoughts constituted less than a minute. I got out of the car. My decision: Walk to the call box. I did. Nothing.

kingdom authority

Couldn't get through between cutoffs and busy signals. I decided to take my chances and walk to a telephone where I could call Anna. This in itself became an epic. (Can you imagine an intersection with three gas stations and one restaurant and not one public telephone within a half mile!) Then . . . a man in front of his house. Would he let a stranger use his phone? He would.

I made contact. One of our guys was on his way to help. Back at my car, I waited as the carousel of thoughts began all over again. *At rush hour, how long everything takes . . . The dinner time is getting too, too close . . . Can I be ready? . . . Don't want this first one to be sloppy . . . What if things fall completely apart? What if . . . Hey, WAIT! Stop worrying, Hayford! Pray!*

And I began to do that.

Stepping behind the guardrail about twenty yards ahead of my car, I began to walk beside the foliage, consulting the Lord for His solution to the time pressure, the needed readiness of things for our church family dinnertime, and my dilemma.

Soon, before anyone else arrived, He did. Peace and confidence began to well up. And then I noticed something.

Junk. Rubbish. Bottles. Trash.

That pretty segment of the freeway I travel daily, with greenery and flowered branches, was thickly packed with broken glass, twisted metal, and dried garbage.

Junk.

It didn't smell, nor was it dangerous. It was just unsightly, but not really noticed until you're stuck beside it going nowhere and in a hurry. And I thought . . .

I thought, *Here I am, helpless, waiting between a roar of traffic on one side and a thicket of trash on the other. But feet away, a fence divides me from a world of people. People, people everywhere and not a soul to . . . but wait. There was One who cared. And while talking with Him, I received direction, confidence, peace and . . .*

flow from His

It struck me. How many of us get stuck just like that.

Not on a freeway nor with a flat tire. But stuck in a life-situation where everything is flying by on one hand and a tangle of trash sits on the other. People nearby are too hurried or seemingly indifferent. You know help is on the way, but you're pressed with demands to get going. . . . Duty snaps its command, and your peace is evaporated. And then you think to step behind His guardrail . . . to pray.

Maybe this true-story-parable is an encouragement. I hope so, because in my situation, betwixt racing cars and rubbish, I prayed. Help arrived. We fixed the tire. And I got there on time (though windblown).

The rush and the trash didn't win after all.

There's a message there somewhere.

Pilgrimage to Plato Center

The Illinois landscape stretching before me looked like cinnamon toast spread with persimmon jelly. Autumn does incredible things to the already lovely countryside, spreading it with color, which alone ought to be convincing proof for the existence of a Creator. The suburban Chicago tollway over which I drove in my rented car, had concluded with the arrival of the farming country. Now the four-lane highway narrowed to two, and the sign beside the fork to the left read, *Plato Center.*

I had come here on purpose, drawn by the memory

of a concrete-post road sign I had driven by twenty-four years before. Anna and I were young in public ministry, following an itinerary from church to church throughout the Great Lakes region, ministering to youth. It was in early spring when our path came to the intersection I was now approaching in the fall of the year, nearly a quarter-century later.

"Plato Center," I remember saying to Anna. "It sounds so distant—so unreal. Like a remnant of another era." We had needed to drive on, unable by reason of schedule to turn aside the one mile indicated to see a town I had never heard of before, but was never to forget: Plato Center, Illinois.

Now my business in the Chicago area offered a one-day hiatus. It was Wednesday, and with no immediate assignment pressing, I decided to pursue my memory. I wasn't even clear as to exactly where that road marker had popped up that springtime long ago. I only remembered it was northern Illinois . . . somewhere on the distant perimeter of Chicago . . . to the west.

And I found it. The town whose name had been engraved on my mind was now passing beside my car. Two dozen houses . . . a gas station . . . schoolhouse . . . one store . . . all sandwiched between the black loam fields on all sides—many already plowed under, although much late feed corn still stood dry on the stalks in perfect road-wide rows. And the church house. Only one. Methodist. With a graveyard across the road.

I tried the church door, wanting to enter, but no one was around. I had decided early that day what I would do if and when I found this town. I would pray . . . I would pray for America.

It was Wednesday, when my congregation, half a continent away, would be joining me around the throne of the Most High God. We would seek His face again, with

repentance and prayer for our sinful nation, which needs forgiveness for its sinning, deliverance from its perverse ways, and healing for its wounds realized through blind excursions into rebellion. I did pray. But it was hard to feel the impact of sin on our land in Plato Center . . . until I walked through the graveyard.

The lawn, tailored nicely around the monuments and headstones there, was strewn with painted leaves—crisp and crunchy under my feet. The engraved names and dates marked the remembrance of people living in the early 1800s—nearly to the founding of our nation. And Romans 5:21 (KJV) came to mind: ". . . Sin hath reigned unto death," a solemn reminder that sin is both a fact of life and a force in history. Even in the rustic beauty and seemingly untainted simplicity of this hidden corner, a message on the need and place of intercession was present.

My pilgrimage to Plato Center was a refreshing reprieve from a busy schedule, and it put my memory of an unvisited site to rest. But it also reminded me of the call to prayer for our land which we have incumbent upon us. Intercession will not remove graveyards from our experience, but it will keep our nation from being buried in our lifetime.

To Pray For a Nation

Most Americans heard the name of Martin Treptow for the first time on a cold Tuesday morning years ago when Ronald Reagan delivered his first inaugural address.

The president quoted from the diary of an American soldier who gave his life in battle in World War I. Unforgettable were the words, "I will do my utmost as if the issue of the whole struggle depended on me alone."

Those words hit me as memorably parallel to the message the Holy Spirit has communicated to our church congregation again and again over the years: *You are to pray as though no other church is praying.*

We have had moments of neglect, I am afraid, but by and large we have stood faithfully at our posts—or knelt there.

We believe the results have been visible, and we are encouraged to move back into the trenches of spiritual warfare as day after day brings reports of victories and advances—as well as new lines of battle.

The facts of God's eternal Word indicate that such praying is not only valid, but that it is also (1) *commanded* by God, (2) *invited* by His promises, (3) *enabled* by His Spirit, and (4) *fruitful* beyond all dreams.

God commands us to pray for nations.

The specific directives of 1 Timothy 2:1-3 and Psalm 2:8 are sufficient to demonstrate that a believer's commitment to prayer at a national and international level springs more from the heart and mind of God than from some fevered fanaticism on the part of the spiritually exuberant. If God *commands* such prayer, believe this: He will answer it! He will move with power because of it, and He won't do anything without it! He *requires* the prayer's partnership, not because His ability is crippled without it, but because His purpose in bringing us to maturity *includes* it.

The promises of the Word invite us.

No passage of God's Word is more fraught with promise than 2 Chronicles 7:14-16. In short, the Lord says that no nation is beyond salvaging, healing, restoring, and delivering—IF *His people will pray.* The follow-up promises in the passage indicate He not only *moves in* to work in that land, but also He will uniquely *dwell* among people who learn to pray that way. And thereby, His dwelling with them will manifest in power and blessing among them!

The Holy Spirit enables intercessors.

We all need to learn to pray in the times we feel we don't know what to say. There are few times like national prayer times that reduce people to speechlessness, to doubt, to the wondering inquiry, "What should I ask for?"

But the Spirit-filled believer is promised help in Romans 8:26-27. The one thing that must be noted, however, is that such assistance only conjoins those who are ready to pray with passion!

Begin by allowing yourself to be stirred with a need: There's a crisis in morality, a crisis in human justice, a crisis in international politics, a crisis in economic mismanagement, a crisis in social decay, a crisis in domestic values. Think! Look at the newspaper, listen to the radio, watch the reports. When you do, let your awareness be turned to prayer passion. Let the Holy Spirit help you take it from there.

The fruit will manifest . . .

. . . As in the classic case of 2 Chronicles 20, when Jehoshaphat called the people to prayer for the nation's deliverance. Fasting with prayer brought victory *then*, and our God, who stands by His promises with an equal availability *today*, awaits your acceptance of the high privilege of prayer and sharing in its power to determine national issues.

Qualifying as An Intercessor

A number of years ago our church family felt called of God to begin a consistent ministry of prayer for our nation and its concerns. Wanting so deeply to be used by our Lord in this effort, we wrestled with a number of "points for repentance" to prepare our hearts for prayer.

I don't list these basic characteristics of an intercessor so that anyone can claim perfection or now-I've-arrived holiness, but rather to encourage a thoroughgoing humility of heart and openness before God.

Second Chronicles 7:14 clearly requires that I *confess* my sinning, that I *humble* myself before God, and that I *turn* from my wicked (warped, twisted out of shape) ways.

Charles Finney, the great evangelist of the nineteenth century, said of repentance: "It implies an intellectual and hearty giving up of all controversy with God upon all and every point . . . a thorough and hearty abandonment of all excuses and apologies for sin."

The wisest believer is that one who comes open-hearted for cleansing, and who knows that God's summons to repentance (a progressive alteration of my way of thought, attitudes of mind, and inclinations of heart) is a *gracious* summons. He invites us to cleansing and forgiveness, but *not* to self-condemnation or a death-dealing despair.

In other words, introspection and confession are to

release us . . . and that release opens the door for bold, history-shaping, nation-changing intercession. Take these points in prayerful transparency before the Lord. Let us be rid of every hindrance so that our boldness in prayer will not be limited.

Study these references and pray,

Father, keep me from any vestige of . . .

1. Religious pride and self-righteousness (Matthew 6:5-6, Luke 18:10-14);

2. Self-will, selfishness, covetousness (Matthew 6:19-21, James 4:3);

3. Faithlessness, doubt, unbelief, anxiety (James 1:5-7, Matthew 6:25-34);

4. Not loving, respecting, and applying God's Word (Proverbs 1:28-29, 28:9);

5. Spiritual adulteries, having idols in the heart (Ezekiel 14:3-13, 2 Corinthians 6:14);

6. Unforgiveness, resentment, having a critical spirit (Mark 11:25, Matthew 5:21-26);

7. Family discord, not being a responsible spouse (1 Peter 3:1-7);

8. Not being open and honest with the brethren (James 5:16);

9. Rebellion, being unwilling to be corrected (Proverbs 1:28-31);

10. Not having true concern for the poor and oppressed (Proverbs 21:13, Isaiah 1:15,17).

We are entering great days. I've said it several times lately. I'm more convinced than ever before that our mighty Lord is preparing to do a great work among His people. It is our task—and great joy—to keep step with Him. Following His lead. Hearing His voice.

Ours is the only army in the world that marches on its knees. And what power!

Glorify Christ Jesus.

How to Pray For World Leaders

God has called us to prayer for "all nations." There is no better way than starting at the top.

The other day a friend asked me to write a few words of explanation on the theme "How to pray for world leaders."

As I worked to keep the guidelines brief, I was forced to simply give Scripture references at points where fully developed teachings would be completely appropriate. If you take time with your Bible and the following suggestions, I believe your effectiveness in prayer will deepen.

First: Be convinced that God has placed these leaders in their positions. As to whether they have ruled in evil or righteousness, they will give account, but it is God's sovereignty that has ordained their term of governing nonetheless (Romans 13:1-4).

Second: It is the believer's responsibility to pray for all governmental leaders. Our calling is not to pass judgment on their rule; but, in obedience to God's Word, to enter into prayer with intercessions that order and peace may fill each land (1 Timothy 2:1,2).

Third: Such praying makes possible the rise of righteous rule in any land, for God OVERrules in all things when intercessory prayer prevails (Psalm 75:7-10). Further, such praying pleases God, for it paves the way for fruitful evangelism to take place in each nation (1 Timothy 2:3-4).

the King Maj

Fourth: Let your heart be filled with confidence that prayer will introduce God's overruling hand wherever faithful believers call forth His dominion. "Your will be done on earth as it is in heaven," is a prayer Jesus taught us to pray *now* (Matthew 6:10).

Fifth: Pray for national leaders to be taught by God that the Lord Almighty is the source of their rule. Pray that humility will fill the hearts of kings who learn to fear God (Daniel 4:34-35). Pray that leaders will love their people more than they love themselves; that they will serve as shepherds and not as taskmasters (Micah 6:8; Jeremiah 23:4,5).

Finally: Pray for the family of each national leader. God is able to work wonders in the heart of any man or woman at this practical dimension of daily life. Rightly ordered authority begins in the home—in family relationships. Pray for miracles in the households of world leaders (Philippians 4:22).

It's astounding to realize that we live in an era of almost instant global communication. As children of our heavenly Father, however, we possess something even more astounding: instant communication with the One who made the world and knows the hearts of all its rulers.

First Priority

I felt a tender touch of the Holy Spirit this week. Call it a tap on the shoulder. A whisper.

He seemed to speak quietly to me, nudging me to avert a recurring danger.

It's the danger of becoming so caught up in prayer warfare and faith's pursuits that I neglect simply being "with Jesus."

"If you abide in Me . . . ," He has said.

It's so simple. So clear.

First and *foremost*, Jesus wants us to experience, sustain, and enjoy a personal, intimate walk with Him.

It isn't that He's disinterested in the demands of our daily duty or the pressures of our private world. Far from it. He just knows that the fountainhead of life is *with Him*. He is the Source. Of everything.

Strength for your day. Wisdom for your task. Comfort for your soul. Grace for your battle. Provision for each need. Understanding for each failure. Assistance for every encounter.

Everything.

So today I invite you to come before Him. Much and often. Come before Him with open heart and childlike simplicity. Come with plain talk. With laughter or tears. Come. On your knees, alone, without fanfare, with all candor.

I write these things because I became so concerned in my prayers for "the work of ministry" that I began to feel something of His divine jealousy. He was saying to me, "I want *you* more than I want your *work*."

My calendar was so full, the agenda so packed, the opportunities so many, the need so great . . . that I began to feel crushed in spirit. The way pressure wilts a flower. "Things"—good, important, worthy things—were dominating my thoughts and prayers. So the Holy Spirit tapped me on the shoulder to slow my mind and redirect my gaze.

Today I pray *for* you and *with* you.

There ARE great ministry opportunities before

us—each one of us. These are days of opening doors. And yes, the needs have never been "needier."

But before we move together on all that, we are wise if we each one—alone and apart from one another—move to another place.

Alone with Jesus. In intimate fellowship.

He wants that for us. And when you think about it, nothing of eternal value occurs in your life without it.

Abide in Me, and I in you. As the branch cannot bear fruit of itself, unless it abides in the vine, neither can you, unless you abide in Me. I am the vine, you are the branches. He who abides in Me, and I in him, bears much fruit; for without Me you can do nothing (John 15:4-5).

A Prayer

Lord God, Creator of all, Maker of my heart . . . I bring it to You this morning.

My heart . . . which at various times has been lifted in praise to You, rejoices over Your goodness and giving to me.

My heart . . . which also sometimes cowers in fear before people and problems—when I forget You are bigger than them all—has been stained by meditations unworthy of a child made in Your image. It has been lifted up in pride over attainments accomplished by Your hand alone.

And, Lord, my heart is often hardened as well. I bring

my heart to You this day for softening . . .

. . . like a *child's*, softened to forgive quickly, easily, without judgment, prejudice, bitterness, or resentment;

. . . like a *field*, softened to receive seeds of Your truth, that the fruit of Your Holy Spirit might be produced through my life;

. . . like *clay*, softened, that I might be shaped today more completely into the man or the woman You want me to become.

Forgive my hardness of heart when it results from my own disobedience, neglect, or outright resistance to Your ways.

Deliver me, lest my heart shrink by reason of this dryness and hardening. Flow the rivers of Your life over my heart, and bring it to renewal, O Lord.

And where my heart is hardened simply by the heat of duty, the weariness of work, the attack of enemies, the slings and arrows of the inconsiderate or crude . . . at those points, give me a vision of *Your* heart today, Lord. For although I have wounded Your love by my failures, You have never hardened Your heart against me.

So, dear God, let my heart be softened today in the same way as Yours toward any who have done to me as I have to You. Deliver me from all temptation to smallness or hardness of heart, and fill my life this morning with Your will and Your Word.

Let the words of my mouth and the meditation of my heart be acceptable in Your sight, O LORD, my strength and my redeemer (Psalm 19:14).

Through Christ, our Lord, Amen.

glorified King

Thou, God, Seest Me

I rose in the morning to pray one day,
    In the bloom of the dawn I rejoiced
And my heart skipped lightly before my God
    As His praises in song I voiced.
It was marvelous being caught up in arms
    Which led my dancing soul.
While I thought I would burst for the joy I felt—
    To sing, to play, at my Father's throne,
That morning.

And there was a day that I rose to pray
    And I wrestled my wandering mind.
"Is it sin or self or Satan, dear Lord,
    That works this frustration; a kind
Of labyrinth of thought. I bump into walls
    That stop my persistent pursuit.
I pressed. I reached out for You, Lord, and found
    My hands full of nothing
That morning."

And that birthed the morning I didn't arise.
    My body dictated the word
Which my mind confirmed, while my spirit squirmed
    For your beckoning voice it heard.
"Come, child. Come be with me.
Come now, watch and pray.
Can you not watch one hour with me?"
    But my body said, "Rest."
    And my mind said, "Remember,

You'll not get far when you're like this,
    This morning."

"Now I'm here again, Lord. It's another day,
    And as sure as I am that you hear;
And as glad as I am to be with you, I'll say
    That my heart's somehow tempted to fear.
I fear I'm a failure at prayer. And I fear
    That my stumbling words will not count.
I fear that I'll ne'er be consistent in prayer
    Like the ones who on eagle-wings mount
Each morning."

Then a voice speaks to me:
"Child of dust, I know you,
    And it's you I've invited to be
With me each day, at that time when you pray,
    Whether dancing or weary, you see.
I have never required certain moods of you,
    And so never require them of Me.
But I'll meet you there
    However you are—
We will dance at times
    When your spirit climbs—
Or 'mid wandering thoughts,
    I'll forsake you not—
And when words are bare
    I'll still hear your prayer.
But keep coming, My child.
Good morning."[9]

AUGUST

Prayer

glory, honor, and

Father God,
I give all thanks and praise
to Thee.

Father God,
My hands I humbly raise
to Thee.

For Thy mighty pow'r and love
Amazes me, Amazes me,
and I stand in awe and worship,
Father God.

Because I Believe This

I believe in God the Eternal Father, Creator of all things. By His Word all things are created. By His promise all things are sustained.

Because I believe this, I am never alone. My Father sees me, knows my need, and is committed to my care. Because He is Creator, there is nothing beyond His capacity to provide. My life is surrounded with the guarantee of His adequacy and His supply.

I believe in God the All-righteous One, who is both loving and holy. His love is expressed in infinite mercy. His holiness is manifest in the absolute changelessness of character.

Because I believe this, I am relieved of the fear that I ever need approach Him with condemnation in my times of weakness or failure, for His mercy endures forever. I am sobered by the truth that His holiness disallows my presumption concerning sin. His perfection both summons my growth in His likeness and assures His grace to continue restoring me unto the same.

I believe in God the Almighty Lord, omniscient, omnipresent, and omnipotent. His wisdom and knowledge superintend all things, His presence pervades in and beyond all things, His power sovereignly rules over all things.

Because I believe this, I can rest in the confidence of His wise design and direction in my life, His personal presence accompanying my life, and His strong right arm embracing my life.

With such a Father as this, I can live. His faithfulness is the ground of my faith.

Supporting Scriptures:
Genesis 1:1-2:3; John 1:1-3; Colossians 1:16,17.
Genesis 18:25 (see vv. 20-33), Psalm 136:1-26, Isaiah 57:15, Malachi 3:6.
Exodus 34:5-8; 1 Chronicles 29:11-13; 2 Corinthians 6:12-15; Psalm 103:1-22; Romans 11:33-36; Revelation 4:1-11.

Praise Is Your Pathway

Many times the best way to be certain of the direction you're going is to look back and see where you've been.

Periodically, over the years, the Lord presses specific points upon us—points of truth He seeks us to acknowledge in the ongoing pattern of life. It is to these we turn, as to milestone markers.

Has praise been a hallmark of your life? Has praise been your constant practice? Has your understanding of praise and its role in your life been growing with the passing months and years?

A few basic reminders from Scripture can bring your life back on track. . . .

flow from His

From Acts 16:19-34: *Darkness surrounds this hour as it did Paul and Silas in the Philippian prison. Their praise brought God's hand by an earthquake and out of the night a hopeless jailer was saved. Now, let your praises rise! As you praise continually, spiritual shock waves go out into the world around you. It will bring your release and the release of many into the Kingdom of God.*

From Psalm 26: *Praise is your pathway through the mired circumstances of the present world. Your step will be uncertain and slide unless you recognize that your praises form stepping-stones by which the Father paves your way into the future purpose He has for you.*

From Job 38:4-7: *As the morning stars sang His praise at creation, accompanying His great display of power with their worship, let your voices join with the heavenly song. Praise the Lord. Sing unto the Lord. Sing with your spirit and sing with your understanding, for as you sing praises unto Him, He continues His great creative working . . . and in your midst you shall see the marvelous works of God, the Lord of the new creation.*

"Let's just praise the Lord." Some might suggest this as a rather closed view of things. I disagree. It's the open door to everything, and the pathway God directs us to walk.

Creation Shall Praise Him

The heavens declare the glory of God;
And the firmament shows His handiwork.
Day unto day utters speech,
And night unto night reveals knowledge.

There is no speech nor language
Where their voice is not heard.
Their line has gone out through all the earth,
And their words to the end of the world
　　　　(Psalm 19:1-4).

It's easy to take something like the simple singing of birds for granted.

In a nature film I watched last week, a group of ornithologists took those songs very seriously. Their conclusions both delighted and disappointed me.

These were scientists who both studied creation and denied their Creator. Their love for our wonderful world was so commendable; their neglect, if not rejection, of our wonderful Lord, so disappointing.

My mind was ignited by one observation they made, fired with an idea which no one could deny as a possibility—not even my bird-watching friends.

My idea was generated by one conclusion their study had drawn. Showing by scientific means that each type of bird renders a distinct call which identifies its kind, the researcher noted, "Here, the bird is saying, *'I'm a red-winged blackbird. I'm a red-winged blackbird.'*"

Of added and striking interest was the fact that each bird has a kind of unique "signature" to the call which identifies its breed; an ending which, in a way, says: *"I am this PARTICULAR red-winged blackbird."*

I turned to Anna and said, "I'm going to challenge the conclusion made by that scientist. His observations are verifiable and enlightening, but he has concluded that the bird is saying, 'I'm a red-winged blackbird.' The fact is, he doesn't know anything more than that the specific call is the identifying song of that specie. My proposition—no less provable than his—is that the birdsong is, *'Praise You, Father, that You created me a red-winged blackbird!'*"

I hold that the evidence of Scripture shows most of creation still in tune with its Creator.

This was verified by one of my first truly exciting discoveries in the Greek New Testament years ago. I was studying the Gospel of John, chapter 1, when in verse 11 I discovered a difference in the gender of the term "His own." The verse reads, "He came unto his own, and his own received him not" (KJV). But the first "His own" has a neuter ending, while the second has a masculine ending. Most literally translated, it would read: "He came unto *His own things* (the whole creation which verse 3 and 10 declare Him responsible for making), and *His own mankind* did not receive Him."

In one sentence the stark fact stands out: Humans are the only beings in the physical realm of this planet who are out of touch with their Creator.

Romans 1:20 tells us that, "Since the creation of the world His invisible attributes are clearly seen, being understood by the things that are made, even His eternal power and Godhead. . . . " But the ensuing verses of that chapter outline the decadence of man and civilization when thanksgiving and honor toward the Almighty are abandoned.

I'm glad I know Him!

I'm glad He made me *me*.

And I'm thankful that through Christ Jesus, the One who made all things, I am being recovered from the debris of confusion in a world where most of humankind have lost their identity and their destined individuality.

It's enough to wake you up in the morning with a song.

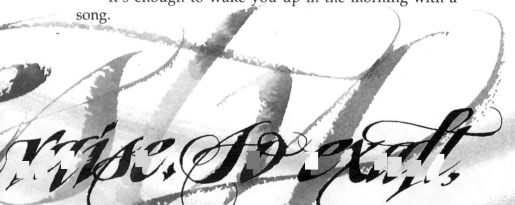

In the Presence of Praise

We who were fathered by the God who spoke all things into existence and who were redeemed by Him who is called the "Word" ought to be aware that what we *say* is phenomenally powerful.

So is what we *don't* say.

Among the disciplines Jesus introduces to our lives is a new sense of responsibility for the words that cross the threshold of our lips. This is no mere attempt at curbing habits of sour gossip. Rather, this is an orientation to a mighty fact concerning our potential as sons and daughters of God.

The words of those alive by God's Spirit are shaping forces. They create, bind up, release . . . and destroy. A full body of biblical text-support can be marshaled to verify this fact. Peter states it tersely in 1 Peter 4:11: "If anyone speaks, let him speak as the oracles of God."

Don't let "the oracles" mystify you. It essentially means we are God's spokesmen . . . His "mouthpiece," if you please. That ought to summon a good deal of silence on our part, wouldn't you think?

God does not waste words. He does not express anything unintended or untimely. He does not misstate Himself. He does not stutter. His Word shatters darkness with light, smashes death with life, and burns sin with fire. Drivel is uncharacteristic of deity. He who is eternal will not lend His Creator-tongue to that which is trivial or frothy.

lift up on high

You and I, then, must speak like sons and daughters of the Most High. We must not dilute the force of our words with empty talk. "Let your speech always be with grace, seasoned with salt" (Colossians 4:6).

In view of these injunctions against careless speaking, why should we place such an emphasis on praise?

Because praise is Scriptural. . . . The Book of Psalms is both guide and handbook for those who would perform God's will in worship. Over 150 times in that book, praise is either enjoined or a commitment to praise is announced. Praise is not a matter of cultural taste, but of wise response to the eternal Word of God.

Because praise is practical. . . . It not only establishes obedience before the Lord, it also releases the worshiper from a host of binding factors that man by nature tends to become subject to: fear, bitterness, hostility, resentment, doubt, and guilt. These and other common limitations begin to fade in the presence of praise.

Because praise is physical. . . . How our flesh quails when first invited to commit itself in open-hearted praise. In Romans 12:1, we are summoned to "present [our] bodies" in spiritual worship to God. Upraised hands and heads are united with uplifted voices in tasteful praise. Psalm 63:3 and 4, 1 Timothy 2:8, and many other texts invite worshipers to manifested as well as meaningful praise.

Let us respond simply. And let us simply respond.

In a world so polluted with empty, foolish, and hurtful words, let's fill our hearts and homes, our workplaces and worship houses with a cleansing current of praise.

Making Your Home A Worship Center

As biblical, stimulating, and renewing as worship with the assembly is, God wants *your home* to be a center of worship as well.

How does that happen? Allow me to offer a few practical guidelines to enhance the spiritual atmosphere where you live.

Kneel.

Yes, kneel! Kneeling is an acknowledged point of submission. It is a way to bring *anything* under Christ's dominion. Kneel as you begin the day: "Lord, this home is Yours for this day." That doesn't substitute for devotional praying, but it's a good way to start the day at your house under Jesus' Lordship (Philippians 2:9-11).

When frustrations rise, anger stirs, bitterness simmers, fear creeps in, and the unexpected crashes in on you, make *kneeling* your retaliation.

Sing.

Not much need to elaborate here. Just do it. Fill your house with song. Tapes and CDs are good, but *don't always* have others doing the praising for you. Sing . . . and keep it up.

Invite Him to dinner.

I abhor "religiousness" in homes. Few children have survived formulated religiosity—packaged, pompous piety. So when I say "worship at the table," I am not

Magnify, come

proposing holding a dinner service while the mashed potatoes chill and a film forms on the gravy. But *do* make your table prayer special; *do* have a part of your table talk related to the Lord's working in each family member's life; *do* keep spiritual reality "natural" to the family circle; *do* sing together (and laugh and cry and worship in the Spirit). Yes. Do.

Have communion.

The elements of the Lord's Supper ought, I believe, to be available in every home. I do *not* recommend such common use of this New Testament privilege that it becomes glib or meaningless, and all should be aware that Scripture gives firm warnings to those who partake in "an unworthy manner." Sensitivity, sobriety of mood, scripturality of participation—all these factors ought to be observed.

Pray . . . while feeding on the Word.

Personal practice of devotions is obviously essential. Family times of sharing in the Word and prayer are great, too—if they are *alive!* I personally prefer using my parental influence to lead my children in cultivating their own *private* devotional life on a daily basis, while family prayer and reading the Word are occasional rather than daily.

As each one in the family grows, sharing your *answers* to prayer and your *discoveries* in the Word becomes enriching to all.

The home as worship center . . . think on that idea. Better still, *act* on it.

What a heritage to pass along to our children . . . memories of home intertwined with memories of praise and laughter and song and the strong, undergirding arms of the living God.

You've Never Seen Me at the Table

Well, at least most of you haven't.

And I should have said you've never seen *us*, because what I meant by "me" was "me with my family." It's something to see . . . a rather unusual experience, to say the least.

We have quite a time together at dinner. It's probably the principal time that we all have together on a consistent basis. The evening meal has become almost sacred—that is, in terms of *importance* . . . but not in terms of *deportment*.

Our deportment, or general manner, is something else. We laugh, eat, joke, praise, correct, teach, play games, laugh some more, tell on each other, joke, praise, correct, teach, play games, laugh some more, tell on each other, eat some more, laugh again, communicate, talk about Jesus, make noise, keep eating (sometimes while talking), correct (for talking with your mouth full), laugh (at the noise from talking with your mouth full), and praise the Lord some more (for having our mouths full—of praise, joy, food, drink—and for our hands filled with each other's hands; we join them when we pray at the start).

Why this rather bouncing description of Hayford table-time?

Because there's something powerfully grand about the potential of a family at table. At least I've found it so; and I believe that God must too, for the Word is chock-full of events surrounding a table.

the King Maj

God built feasts into the worship calendar of Israel.

Jesus taught regularly from a banquet table.

David's praise to the Lord God, the Great Shepherd, centered on His faithfulness to feed His sheep—in green pastures . . . and to prepare a table before him in the time his enemy would surround him.

At the end of time, Scripture shows God's people gathered at a table. Revelation 19 answers to Jesus' words in Matthew 26, when He spoke of His high anticipation of the day when He will drink wine with us in His Father's Kingdom.

The people of God eat often . . . and *together*.

There it is. That's what I'm after. I want you to think about our eating together.

I want you to think about setting an extra place or two at your dinner table. Often. There are those without family circles whose suppers tonight will be lonely, joyless affairs. You know who I'm talking about. Singles. Foreign students. Elderly folks. Maybe a young couple feeling rootless and far from home.

For one night, your family circle could become theirs.

I'm not talking about a roast served on china and everybody feeling stiff and uncomfortable. I'm talking about meatloaf served on your old comfortable dishes to a family in their old comfortable clothes. I'm talking about letting folks join your tribe for an hour or two, while everyone takes the risk of just being themselves.

Scripture says, "God sets the solitary in families" (Psalm 68:6).

How about yours?

How about tonight?

The A-B-Cs of Praise

I was at my devotional prayertime in New Orleans last Wednesday morning, and as I began to praise the Lord, my heart was filled with a simple idea which overflowed as I responded to the Holy Spirit's stirring.

In beginning to worship God, I was prompted with the thought of expressing praise to Him through every letter of the alphabet. Matching each letter with one of His attributes, I began with "A" and found myself at "Z" in very short order. It came so readily and naturally I knew His Spirit was assisting my praise. I thought my little "primer" might be encouragement and stimulus for your own private moments of worship.

Lord God, I lift my heart to You because the richness of Your person commands my highest devotion. I praise You because You are . . .

ALMIGHTY—There is no power that exceeds Yours.

BEAUTIFUL—The loveliness of Your Being is displayed in Your handiwork in Creation and Your heart-gift of the Lord Jesus.

CREATOR—You are never limited by what is. You can always do more than seems possible.

DEPENDABLE—I never face a situation without the assurance that You are there.

EVERLASTING—You encompass my very being with Your breath of life and love.

FULFILLER—Your Spirit causes me to overflow with hope and enables me for living.

GLORIOUS—You pour radiance into the ordinary.

HOLY—The awesome completeness of Your Being brings new dimension to mine.

IMMUTABLE—Your unchanging nature comforts me in a world of constant change and decay.

JEHOVAH—Your chosen Name expresses Your all-sufficiency given to me.

KIND—As a loving father takes time for his children, so do You.

LOVING—Beyond human description or grasp, this is true.

MINDFUL—Your Word says You are always thinking about me. I'm overwhelmed.

NEW—In Your gift of mercies every morning and in Your working of constant "new things."

OMNIPOTENT—Whatever tests my faith, Your limitless mightiness is my reservoir of strength.

PRECIOUS—Your Word is like gold, and Your presence is treasured.

QUICK—You do not unnecessarily delay, but always answer me at the best time.

RIGHTEOUS—Your justice, fairness, and even-handedness deal life to us all with faithful lovingkindness.

SENSITIVE—Your heart is touched with my feelings . . . You care.

TERRIFYING—Not to me, Lord, but to the Enemy—he flees before You.

UNDERGIRDING—Your strong arm supports me always, in all ways.

VICTOR—The triumph You have won over all life and death is given to me, too!

WONDERFUL—Not only in Your character, but in Your full-of-wonder doings.

EX-CELLENT—Your ways and Your Being transcend my highest imaginings.

YESTERDAY, TODAY, and FOREVER—Assuring me that every issue of my past, present, and future is under Your covering.

ZESTFUL—Life has no dull moments when I live it with You!

Praise Him with me!

I was astounded sometime back to learn that our English word "worship" has its root in the word *worth*.

It began to unfold in my understanding. Real worship of God isn't the exercise of a religious ritual, it is the *reflection of a proper value judgment* formed by a man about God. I most honor the God who created me and the Lord Jesus who redeemed me, when I ascribe the right value to Him.

He's *worth* my praise, adoration, and exaltation. How then do I make my worship "worthy" . . . substantial in quality?

The New Testament word "worthy" or "worth" occurs forty-one times in the form of the Greek term *axios*, which basically refers to "weight." It related to a time when people did business with coins that were minted in the exact amount of the precious metal which the coin declared to be its value. To use our own history as an example, a twenty-dollar gold piece was minted of exactly twenty dollars worth of gold. Today our coins only represent a value, they do not comprise it.

In the world of Bible times, those coins used in repeated exchange were subject to wear. Just by passage from hand to hand the coin would diminish in its "worthiness." Consequently, a handful of coins would be weighed to confirm their adequacy of value or to show their insufficiency. In other words, the face value imprinted on the coin was not necessarily a true statement of its worth. The scales told the difference.

How do you prepare for "worthy worship"? Thank God, there *is* a way!

Whatever insufficiency exists in me as a result of being passed from hand to hand, so to speak, like the coin worn by world-wear, He is able to redeem—to revaluate —*by His forgiveness*. He takes the coin drained of "worth" and mints it freshly by filling it with His Spirit. He brings a "weight of glory" that develops people of real substance.

Be reminded today . . .

Worship the Father. Rise above the ritualistic and rejoice in the real.

Praise the Son. His resurrection power raises us to His level of triumph.

Be filled with the Spirit. For that fullness brings weight to the life and a clear ring to the coin with your face on it.

Triumphal Reentry

I saw the King last night, He was reentering the gates,
    But the scene somehow was different than before.
There were praising hosts and children singing loud hosannas there,
    As He passed in triumph through Jerusalem's door.

But their hands did not hold branches and their coats were not cast down,
    And the King did not an ass's colt employ.
But each greeter held a trumpet, and their glist'ning garments wore
    Lifting praise to Him whose entry all enjoyed.

And the King was on a stallion white, a mighty prancing steed,
    And a glorious air the greeters' voices raised:
"Hail the Conquering One, King Jesus, who has gone forth conquering—
    King of Glory, enter now these gates called Praise."

Then I knew it was a vision—calling me beyond my view,
    Which till then was bound to past or future planes:
Until now "Triumphal Entry" only spoke of history,
    Or of prophecy when Jesus comes again.

Only spoke of that Palm Sunday long ago when children sang,
    Or of that day when our once and future King
Shall return in clouds of glory and reenter Zion's gates,
    And as Earth's Redeemer then His Kingdom brings.

But this Holy Spirit vision brought new wonder to my
    soul,
     As His truth like sunrise dawned so gloriously.
He was bringing understanding for our present struggles
    here,
     Off'ring present triumph now for you and me.

So today, behold this vision. Holy Spirit, help us all
    Clearly hear John's Revelation—all it tells.
How that One upon a white horse, charges forward as we
    pray,
     Daily warring, conquering darkest hosts of hell.

"He went conq'ring and to conquer," so the prophecy
    relates,
     And in speaking thus describes repeated wars,
How our Lord who left Jerus'lem after that first Triumph-
    day
     Now through Calv'ry's vict'ry conquers evermore.

Daily comes through gates of glory where pure hearts lift
    up their praise,
     As they face their battles with His triumph-song:
"Hail, King Jesus, Mighty Conq'ror, once the Lamb of
    Calvary,
     Now you've mastered death and evil, sin and
    wrong."

And I saw how as we praise Him, He reenters even now
    Rides to meet His own—just one, or praising throng.
He will enter our Jerus'lem, then go forth—again, again—
    Forth to conquer sin and evil, just as long . . .

Just as long as wise hearts worship, just as long as some
    still know,
    That the battle is not ours, it is the Lord's.
And as praise goes forth, so He does; and new victories
    secures,
    And new triumph scenes become our great reward.

186

So lift ceaseless praise, redeemed ones, singing, "Worthy is the Lamb,
    Who as Judah's Lion roars upon His prey."
His the battle, ours the worship; His the triumph, ours the song;
    His reentry ours to sing at every day.[10]

glory, honor, and

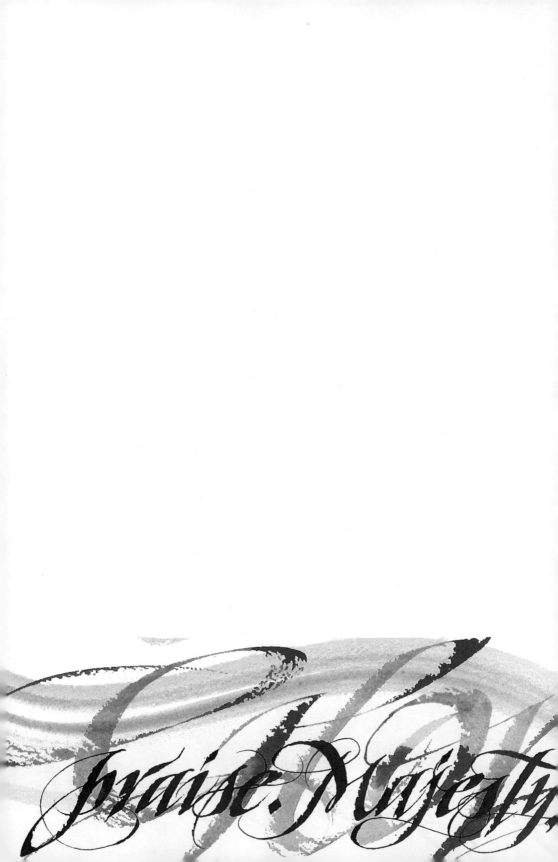

SEPTEMBER

Contemplation

if kingdom authority—

Cleansing power in this hour,
Wash my heart and all sin erase.
Blood of Jesus, flow and free us;
Lead us, Lord, to Thy resting place.

flow from His

On Rembering What You Are Told

I chuckled when a friend recently said, "I have an excellent memory. It's just *short!*"

We all lament our forgetfulness. Memory is a frightening tattletale: It reveals our real and immediate priorities . . . what's most important to me *now*.

This doesn't mean if I forget my wedding anniversary that my marriage or my wife isn't important to me. It just humbles and embarrasses me with the fact that the celebration date came at a time when something else was crowding my mind for prior attention.

That doesn't excuse me for my neglect, nor exempt me from responsibility for being thoughtless. It just catches me with my priorities out of order.

Jesus said, "He that has an ear, let him hear what the Spirit says to the churches" (Revelation 2:7,11,17,29; 3:6,13,22). He says it repeatedly in the letters He dictated to John, and often make very similar statements in His earthly ministry (Matthew 11:15, 13:9,43; Mark 4:9,23; 7:16; and Luke 8:8, 14:35).

It is startling to note that these words—*If you have ears to hear, listen!*—are spoken only by the Lord Jesus. In all the Bible, only He speaks this command. That fact certainly establishes priority, doesn't it?

I can remember a few instances from my childhood when I got in trouble for not doing what I had been told. It wasn't that I didn't listen, it was that I didn't *remember*. Because even we who listen are inclined to forget, Jesus urges us to let His sayings "sink down into [our] ears" (Luke 9:44).

In the coming week, I challenge you to take time to review some of the things God's Spirit has been whispering to your heart over the past six months. We need to be careful to remember what we have been told.

Some of us may need more than a gentle reminder. It might be that the accumulated wax of careless habit needs to be washed away with a stream of Holy Spirit "ear irrigation." People who have had that physical treatment tell me it hurts. The spiritual wash job might hurt, too. But it will be worth it.

Hearing and heeding can save us a great deal of pain.

Divine Adjustments

I don't know anything about watches or clocks.

I'm even mystified by the mechanics I have to go through on a thirty-day month to get my stem-wound calendar watch advanced to where the date and day are both correct.

But I do know that "balance," "adjustment," and "good timing" are three clock-talk terms. They're also three terms that need to come to mind as we are praying.

I made a major calendar adjustment this past week. I was to have spent the whole month of next January ministering in conferences and churches throughout Australia and New Zealand—major cities and many conferences.

The trip had been scheduled for months. I was committed. But something was wrong. The whole thing tied into the same season last spring when I made a whirlwind set of bad decisions. I have since confessed it all to the Lord, and have marveled at how He has compensated, redeemed, covered, and forgiven.

But this particular trip, this residual, lingering remnant of that season remained. It had never occurred to me that it, too, might be wrong.

It was.

Two weeks ago, while I was up early one clear and chilly morning, walking a leaf-strewn back road in Maine, praying and communing with the Lord, He told me.

He didn't slap me in the face with it. But like a Master of timepieces, He gently adjusted something in my understanding. It didn't explode, it didn't introduce a recorded announcement. Nothing dramatic happened. But one small, inner sense was awakened. It stirred—and then stood up and shook violently.

My sense of unsettledness.

I knew something was wrong. If my wristwatch started chiming on my arm it wouldn't have been any clearer. Something was badly out of balance. Out of timing. Out of synch.

Father, I prayed urgently, stirred in the depths of my soul as though an ocean wave had struck, *what's the matter?*

I didn't hear a voice, but I did receive a clear, concise impression. A message from Headquarters. *Pray about the Australia trip.*

I did. I began then and continued for seven days. I

felt freed to ask the heavenly Father to give me firm confirmation as to whether I should go or not.

The events of the days which followed are thrilling to review: (1) the peace in knowing He was going to set the balance and establish timing for the trip; (2) the joy in knowing He never abandons us to our own imperfect planning, but will signal us in time; and (3) the confidence that He would take care of things on both ends. If I went in January, He'd cover all matters at home base in California. If I stayed home, He would supply the ministry needed in Australia and New Zealand.

When the seven days were past, a powerful and precious thing took place. The Lord sent the answer. It was clear. It was sure. It was as finely tuned and perfectly understandable as the time on the face of a clock. The precision of the message brought the confidence you would have in setting your watch by a giant steeple timepiece maintained by a master clockmaker.

Looking back on it all this morning, my heart is filled with praise and thanksgiving to the God who keeps us in time . . . who keeps us adjusted to His will and His way for us.

Unraveling Snafus

"I'm writing," I explained, "to attempt somehow to clear up the confusion that surrounded our recent exchange of notes, calls, attempts at contact, etc."

My letter went on to interpret what had happened. I

hoped it would help, but I didn't expect a cure. Hindsight explanations don't usually seem adequate to unravel the mind-boggling tangles two fallible humans seem capable of at times.

In World War II, the military coined an acronym for it—SNAFU: Situation Normal, All Fouled Up. That's another way of saying, "Wherever people are involved, let's simply adapt ourselves to the necessity of things being messed up."

But that kind of "normalcy" isn't tolerable—especially in relationships. Too many snares snag at the soul already, tearing joy and meaning from our lives. I vote for confronting them all—and I assert that strained, wounded, or broken relationships are primary points of beginning if we are to be truly free.

What to do?

As with my letter, I suggest the following where relationships have been "snafu-ed." Contact—by letter, phone, or in person—might include the following elements:

Affirm your deep sense of value for the person involved. All of us need to be needed. All of us are threatened with a sense of limited worth. All of us feel misunderstood. All of us need bolstering. It isn't a matter of pampering or babying; it's simply a matter of needing to be cared about.

Request the other person's understanding of your own ineptness or failure. You and I are in a stronger position when we acknowledge our helplessness, weakness, and dependence upon the patience of others. In doing so I am not asking people to tolerate my presumptuously *requiring* them to allow me to act and remain infantile. Not at all. But I am saying that my humanity makes for a lot of cracks in my perfection. Rather than building a facade, we need help from patient people in patching up the cracks in the plaster of our personalities. Let's ask for that help.

196

Be patient yourself, if your overtures don't receive an immediate response. Our finest attempts have a way of bouncing back in our faces at times. But believe me, the Holy Spirit can bless the *spirit* of your approach even beyond what your words can do. The *fact* of your attempt provides grounds for His ongoing working.

Don't succumb to the flesh-thought, *I'd better leave well enough alone.* "Snafu" isn't "well enough." Unraveling, like a child's spaghettied shoelaces, often takes time and patience.

Join me, won't you? With our Lord's help, SNAFU *could* mean, "Situation Normal, All *Fixed* Up."

I turned to see the voice that spake with me . . . and his eyes were as a flame of fire (Revelation 1:12, 14, KJV).

In such words, John the exile reported his encounter with the glorified Christ.

As the conversation continued, the Lord of the Church dictated seven letters for the apostle to transcribe and deliver. The resurrected Son of God looked into the soul of His collective people and with purifying eyes aflame, set Himself to purge them.

The basic meaning of the word "purge" expresses something desirable: "to clear of guilt; to free from moral or ceremonial defilement; to make free of an unwanted substance; to relieve or to rid of pressure or sediment."

I experienced a purging this week, realized in direct relationship to a church-wide fast we joined together. One of the objectives of that season of fasting was "the purging and purifying of the Body." Just as the physical body is cleansed by a fast, so we sought a spiritual cleansing as we waited together upon the Lord in fasting and prayer.

My experience began the second day of the fast. I don't know that I can fit it into words, except to say the Lord purged me *right through the eyes*. My perspective changed, and I saw my role as husband and father in a startling new light. After the occurrence of that unexpected, not-even-asked-for moment of truth, I became aware that a veil had been lifted from my eyes. An unrecognized but very real blind spot had suddenly been removed.

It could be that many of you have yet to experience the fruit of prayer-with-fasting. I have a recommendation. As you pray and seek His cleansing, expect the possibility that your own purging will come with respect to the way you *see* . . . a person, a relationship, a task, a call of God, a responsibility, a specific situation.

Follow your fast with a special sense of "looking unto Jesus." When His moment comes, He'll show Himself to you as He did to John. And when His eyes strike yours, He'll burn off the blinders and release insight and vision you've never known before.

Like me, you'll find yourself blinking in the new-found brightness.

The Grace To Be Wrong

I am becoming increasingly sensitive to the need for grace in believers which will allow them to be wrong.

Not to *do* wrong. But to *be* wrong.

There are far too few who simply acknowledge their own humanity when their own doings, calling, efforts, or sincere goals are called into question.

This past week I encountered three occasions where this grace was needed: at a gathering of men who were consulting together over a specific ministry to the Body of Christ; in a conversation over the radio, in which I was being interviewed on the subject of the believer and his willingness to acknowledge his failures; and in a private counseling session in which we discovered a man's preoccupation with his sense of God-given mission, to the point that he couldn't see the need for balance. He was too taken with *his* sense of the importance of what he felt *he* was supposed to do.

Somehow, "being right" isn't as easy as one thinks. Our own sense of dimension on a matter is the key to balance, and the fact is that when something *seems* important or necessary to me, it tends to become ALL important . . . ABSOLUTELY necessary. And the time for the answer to this important/necessary matter is always NOW! Especially if God and His will are involved in the matter.

Thankfully, I am discovering a small but growing

band of folks who are willing to trust the Lord to cover their imperfections—whether it be in timing, in understanding, or in sense of urgency. They are gaining the capacity to be wrong in their *perspective*, as right as they might be in their *purpose*.

I find that grace was powerfully present in the early Church. I hear the apostles and elders at Jerusalem say, concerning a decision that would reshape the Church's future, "It seemed good . . ." (Acts 15:28). Before they invoke the ultimate of divine authority, they simply says, "We thought a lot about it. It seemed good to the Holy Spirit and to us." History confirms the decision they made, but I am most impressed by the non-authoritarian air with which the judgment was communicated.

Paul says twice in 1 Corinthians 7 that his counsel is offered "as a concession, not as a commandment" (v. 6); and that his directives concerning marriage and the single life were "according to [his] judgment" (v. 40). He does affirm that he believed himself to have the mind of the Holy Spirit on the subject, but again, the authority is exercised with wisdom. There is an apparent willingness to hearing others out on the subject.

I love Peter's capacity to not know as much as another brother, and still to love and trust that brother's words toward him. Second Peter 3:15,16 manifests a *readiness to receive* the gift of another's wisdom and expertise, without denying or having to hurriedly insist that you *have received* much already yourself.

Somehow, you and I experience a painful reluctance to utter the words, "I don't know." Or, "I may not be entirely right." Or, "I need your balancing counsel on this, my friend." It's hard for us to say these things *and mean them* with a truly teachable spirit.

Some matters, of course, are not negotiable. But my personal inclinations, however "sure" I might feel about them, must be kept available to modification within the circle of those who love me in Christ.

Such vulnerability is the only safety valve against the recurrent problems which "rugged individualism" has wrought in personal and family lives, in business and government matters, and in the Church of the Lord Jesus throughout history.

Let's keep hands joined in trust. Mine and yours may not be perfectly clean, but keeping hold will sure help us keep our balance.

A Good Reminder About a Bad Heart

In some recent studies of Exodus, I have again been impressed with the frightening capacity of the human heart to resist God. Pharaoh, ruler of Egypt and emperor of the most powerful nation of his time, is a case study which ought to be a good reminder to us all.

Don't make the mistake of supposing yourself incapable of heart-hardness. Jeremiah reminds us that *all* hearts are self-deceiving (Jeremiah 17:9). The lessons distilling from Pharaoh's self-damning mindset make it unnecessary for anyone to make the same mistake. That's why I took care in noting a few observations:

He supposed he knew everything about the Lord.

When Moses first demands Israel's release in the name of the Lord, Pharaoh's "Who is the LORD?" (Exodus 5:2) is more a smart-aleck remark than a question. He says in essence, "There's nothing about *that* God that I don't know or can't beat."

My spirit may not be the same as Pharaoh's, but I need to guard against the presumption that because I *know* the Lord, that I know *all* about Him that I need to know. Heart-hardness is the price of presumed knowledge. A humble heart is characterized by confessed ignorance and teachability.

He was unaffected though surrounded by the miraculous.

If there is anything miracles do *not* guarantee, it is obedient faith. The alarming capacity of the human heart to behold the power of God and still remain unchanged is terrible in its potential. Pharaoh watched Moses' rod become a serpent, consume the magicians' rods, and then become a rod again in Moses' hand. He saw the Nile turned to blood. He saw plagues devastate his nation while Israel was protected through divine intervention, and STILL "he hardened his heart" (8:15, 32).

What evidences of God's power do *you* see as you look around you? You and I are surrounded by phenomenal displays of God's power, grace, and miraculous operations. Yet unbelief and thanklessness survive too easily. Beware, my heart!

He was finally given over to his own devices.

When the Bible says, "The LORD hardened the heart of Pharaoh" (9:12), we are not dealing with a case of predestined destruction. Let no one misunderstand the Lord's forecast of this occasion (4:21, 7:3). To the contrary, God never predestines a person's failure, even when His prescience foresees it. Exodus 9:16 makes clear that God raised Pharaoh up with the possibility of becoming one of the most remarkable rulers ever. He might to this day be remembered as the Great Emancipator, had he taken his hour of opportunity responsibly and obediently before God.

But . . . the sad fact of history is that Pharaoh repeatedly *hardened his own heart* until God finally said, "Then have it your way!"

The Holy Spirit has a gentle yet pointed way of dealing with each of us. Lessons like this, from the eternal Word of God, serve as a strong warning as well as a comforting assurance: If I keep my heart humble before God, I can be certain of His highest purposes being realized in my life.

That's the kind of heart I want.

Always.

Keeping House Isn't Romantic

Most believers face a hurdle called "romanticism" in the course of their growth in the Lord Jesus. You and I must find a way to leap that hurdle . . . or be tripped up again and again.

I didn't say that a deeply emotional or sentimental feeling toward our Lord is *wrong*. It isn't. Such feelings should never be lost. They're a part of retaining that "first love" which He seeks in the simplicity of our worship, walk, and service.

But there is a thoughtless giddiness sometimes found in folks like any of the best of us. It is usually evident in those who have freshly tasted the new wine of life in Christ—a Christianity that has been stripped of the nonessentials of ritualism, religion, and doctrinaire attitudes which reduce life to form and remove joy from experience.

It's heady stuff, new wine. It will make you suppose that everything is coming up roses. That's not bad when everything *really is* coming up roses. But not everything that rises in the midst of a freshly sown garden is fruitful. Even the best gardens have weeds.

Over the years I've noticed a certain weediness of mind among people freshly aglow from revival's fires. Unfortunately, the fire doesn't consume the weeds. In fact, at times it seems the heat encourages their growth. These weeds have a way of diminishing the possibilities of fruit-fulness in the newly ignited.

Excitement is mistaken for growth.

Information is mistaken for understanding.

Sentimental feelings are mistaken for true commitment.

Having the "feel-goods," hearing the latest teaching tape, or attending the latest Christian seminar has little to do with maturity. And no "word from the Lord" or singing "O, How I Love Jesus" will substitute for abiding commitment.

Maturity and commitment are durables. As desirable and proper-in-place as the excitement, the hearing of stir-ring truth, or the romantic might be, they are each only introductory. They are starting places toward deeper maturity and firmer resolve.

Every romance, to become a deepening relationship, must come to the point of accepting responsibility for "set-ting up house." This involves accepting the commitment of marriage, assuming certain duties, and attending to certain details. Does this mean that you lose the electric thrill of the merely "romantic"? Perhaps. But you don't lose love. In fact, love is given a new dimension in which to mature.

You and I are wise to think through this distinction in our churches. Are we *only* a "revival church," or are we a

204

revival people, constantly deepening in our maturity and our capacity to accept the responsibility involved in true commitment?

Romance is fine. Flowers and candles and goosebumps have their place. But it is commitment that binds the wounds, pays the bills, stands the heat, and hangs in there regardless of the cost.

The former sounds like a fling. The latter sounds like love.

A Test of Commitment

Maybe it was a legalistic pressure point imposed upon me by some churchiness to which I was exposed in my upbringing, but carrying one's Bible always was important.

We had Sunday school awards and point systems that scored you higher if you had your own Bible with you.

In church, a Bible in the hymnal rack was the sign of a rather "backslidden" church . . . I mean, why didn't the people bring their own, anyway?

At school, the "gutsy Christians" were the ones who carried their Bible along with their books. It was a kind of declaration of where you stood.

Carrying your Bible on the way to church was "good style." "Don't be caught without your sword," we were taught. And it stuck. I carry my Bible with me a lot of the time. Just to have it handy. "Never know when you'll need it," you know.

Having your Bible around was kind of like being unafraid to bow your head in a restaurant. You weren't like you "used to be," when you scratched your eyebrows as you prayed over the food. You know, in case someone was watching, you wouldn't look "weird."

Well, years come and go, and sometimes I wonder what progress really is. I've grown a lot in the Lord, and I think I'm unafraid to stand up for Him when the chips are down.

But the other day, I left my Bible in the car when I was going into a restaurant.

Wait a minute. Hear the whole thing. I was going in there to the banquet room to speak to a group of people about Jesus.

Right. I was the speaker . . . on a Bible theme . . . uh-huh. And I left my Bible in the car.

Now, there's more to it than that. They had printed outlines with the entire text I was going to speak from already in hand. I knew they would. So I didn't *really* need my Bible.

What bothers me is how comfortable I felt about that. The convenient sense of a somewhat carnal ease which I felt when I got out of the car. The fact is, I was slightly relieved.

Well, anyway, I guess it's a mark of maturity to not want to appear too religious.

Or is it cowardice?

All I know is I'm carrying my Bible a little more openly nowadays. I mean, if you're truly filled with the power of the Dove, you certainly shouldn't grow older and find yourself chicken.

Teach Me About Thy Cross

Teach me about Thy Cross, dear Lord,
    nothing presumed, I've all to learn.
Spirit of God, unfold the Word;
    Thy deepest secrets let me learn.

Prone to indulge my selfish whims;
    failing to learn Thy purity.
Bent on my will, my pride, my sins;
    teach of Thy Cross and liberate me.

Make of Thy Cross a yoke for me;
    crowd me toward life, all sin erase.
Discipline every energy,
    Lord, may Thy glory shine on my face.

Jesus, Thy Cross all pow'r has gained;
    sin, death, and hell now vanquished lay.
May I by faith that vict'ry claim,
    and in Thy triumph reign every day.

No earth or hell can e'er compete
    I now am loosed, who once was bound.
Serpents and scorpions 'neath my feet;
    Christ's conq'ring glory shines all around.[11]

Unto Jesus be

glory, honor, and

Praise Majesty

OCTOBER

Faith

kingdom authority–

Since Jesus rules in me
I'm filled with His beauty;
Now it's my duty
To live like a chosen one.

flow from His

No Accidents

I'll call her Ginny. She sat in my office, completely stunned. Bewildered.

"Pastor Jack, I feel kind of dumb but—this has really jarred me. I just found out from my mother that I was conceived before my folks married. In fact, I'm the only reason they *did* marry. Suddenly, here in my mid-twenties, I'm facing some hard facts. One, I wasn't planned. Two, I wasn't desired. And three, I was an accident that forced a marriage which finally broke up anyway. Pastor, this may sound stupid, but I really need help in knowing how to think about myself."

I've heard Ginny's lament phrased in many different ways through the years. It's no wonder. Even our public education system programs boys and girls to think of themselves as "accidents" in the history of the universe—spawned by cosmic chance rather than pur-posed by divine and special creation.

I knew better when talking to Ginny that day, and as I pen these words, I'm wondering if *your* day has brought such questions to mind.

"Everything's so messed up. Does anything about me right now really make sense?"

"Is there a purpose to me—for me? Is there any reason for my life, my job, my relationships—or am I just driftwood in the sea of humanity?"

Let me tell you what I told Ginny that day in my office. What I'm about to offer is more than just a collection of inspirational thoughts or some philosophical theory. It is the very heartbeat of God's changeless, utterly reliable Word.

"Ginny," I said, "you've received some bad news. But I've got good news about you. It's written in God's letter to us all, His Word of Truth—the Bible. Listen to what He says . . .

Before I formed you in the womb I knew you; Before you were born I sanctified you [or, set you apart for Myself] . . . (Jeremiah 1:5).

"Hear the prayer of David . . .

> *You made all the delicate, inner parts of my body, and knit them together in my mother's womb. Thank you for making me so wonderfully complex! It is amazing to think about. Your workmanship is marvelous—and how well I know it. You were there while I was being formed in utter seclusion! You saw me before I was born and scheduled each day of my life before I began to breathe. Every day was recorded in your Book!*

> *How precious it is, Lord, to realize that you are thinking about me constantly! I can't even count how many times a day your thoughts turn towards me. And when I waken in the morning, you are still thinking of me! (Psalm 139:13-18, TLB).*

"Ginny," I continued, "I want you to hold on to these three thoughts when you walk through that office door. First, God had you in mind before your parents even met. Second, He planned on you before you were born. And third, He has beautiful plans for your future from now on."

Our conversation went on longer, but it's enough for now to say she left my office a free woman. Free from the fear of pointlessness. Free from feelings that nobody cared.

If there's anything God's Word wants us to know, that's it: The mighty Creator of everything says, "I know all about you. I care about you. I can help you right now, right where you are, if you'll ask Me to."

Your situation may be unlike Ginny's, but we all need to hear God's Word to us:

For I know the plans I have for you, says the Lord. They are plans for good and not for evil, to give you a future and a hope (Jeremiah 29:11, TLB).

That beats both nagging fears and empty humanistic philosophy. God says, "You're not an accident. Your existence is not a mistake. I have designed you on purpose, no matter what anybody thinks . . . *including you*."

Sleep on that tonight. It will give you something to get up for in the morning.

What's Happening When Nothing Seems to Be

How many times have you prayed, knowing full well that you have put the matter before God in faith, resting upon His Word . . . and then nothing happens?

Before long, a rash of possible explanations or procedures tempt you:

- Doubt—"Maybe God hasn't heard me."

- Fear—"Maybe He has heard me, but doesn't want to do anything about it."

- Uncertainty—"Perhaps it isn't God's will (except I was *so sure* when I prayed)."

- Condemnation—"It's probably because I don't deserve an answer. I've failed often enough that I can't blame God for turning away from me, occasionally."

- Haste—"I've waited long enough, I guess God just wants *me* to be the answer. I'll just barge into the situation on my own and do my best."

- Presumption—"The key is to demonstrate my faith, so I'll act like everything has changed and treat the situation as though it were accomplished."

We live in an instant credit, get-everything-now economy. We eat add-water-and-mix foods or drive by fast-food outlets which poke our palates with immediate delicacies ranging from burgers and burritos to fried chicken and fish 'n' chips. All of this trains us to want what we want *now* on the basis of something that requires little or nothing of us. We don't grow trees in our yards, we buy them potted and several years advanced in their growth—or move to another house where they're already grown.

Waiting is not in style, and patience has never been a forte of the flesh.

But the Word of God has a great deal to say about "waiting." Sample some of the truth . . .

Indeed, let no one who waits on You be ashamed;
Let those be ashamed who deal treacherously without
*   cause. . . .*

Lead me in Your truth and teach me,
For You are the God of my salvation;
On You I wait all the day. . . .

Let integrity and uprightness preserve me,
For I wait for You. . . .

Wait on the LORD;
Be of good courage,
And He shall strengthen your heart;
Wait, I say, on the LORD! . . .

I will praise You forever,
Because You have done it;
And in the presence of Your saints
I will wait on Your name, for it is good. . . .

O You his Strength, I will wait for You.
For God is my defense . . .

My soul, wait silently for God alone,
For my expectation is from Him
(Psalms 25:3,5,21; 27:14; 52:9; 59:9; 62:5).

These verses represent but a simple start on the theme—and only from one book in the Bible. Try Psalm 69 for size. Read of a heart crying for a long-awaited answer . . . and how faith eventually rises in the face of fear, doubt, impatience, and questioning.

If God wasn't *growing* sons and daughters, things would not take nearly as long. But since He is more interested in our *growth* than He is in our *getting*, waiting becomes a very essential and useful means toward that end. He doesn't traffic in add-water-and-mix saints, or in freezer-to-microwave-to-table kids. He builds with neither plastic nor papier-maché.

What do you do, then, while you're waiting?

Know that He isn't teasing you.

Be confident that He takes no delight in compelling you to wait. He is, rather, patiently overseeing your life. He doesn't want you to drown while you're still learning to swim.

Rest . . . for He wants you to trust Him.

When nothing seems to be happening, something really is! You're facing a new opportunity for learning faith—the kind that grows, not just "gets."

I Believe In Jesus Christ

I believe in Jesus Christ the Son of God; the Word, who was one with the Father before all worlds; the Love Gift of the Father for the redemption of this world; and the One in whom the Father is pleased to have all fullness dwell now and forever.

Because I believe this, I worship Him as Alpha and Omega—the Beginning and the End—for He precedes all and exceeds all that has or shall ever be. I receive and acknowledge Him as Redeemer, for He alone is adequate to furnish release and salvation for mankind. I honor Him as Lord above all, according to the Father's desire that every knee bow and every tongue confess His name with praise.

I believe in Jesus Christ the sinless Savior; the Word made flesh through virgin birth, and a body thereby prepared for sacrifice as the Lamb of God to take away the sins of the world. I believe that in His death He bore the full weight and consequence of all our sins, that we through His blood might be justified before God, forgiven and cleansed in heart and conscience, and progressively purified in holiness of life.

Because I believe this, I welcome the personal triumph in life that is mine because Jesus Christ has come in the flesh: I acknowledge Him as my substitute in payment for my sins; I accept the divine release from all guilt or condemnation, since because of Jesus, the Father's accounts show me as never having sinned; and I commit myself to Him who gave His life for me,

Magnify, come

that He may live His life daily through mine, in thought, word, and deed.

I believe in Jesus Christ the living Lord; resurrected from the dead, a victor over hell's every power, ascended to the Father's right hand, ruling in might, and ceaselessly interceding for His own.

Because I believe this, I walk in victory by faith in Him; free of fear, delivered from darkness, secured by His power, reigning with Him in life, and sustained by His constant watch over me.

With such a Master as this, I can live in the confidence that all He has begun in me He will complete—unto the day of His return.

Supporting Scriptures:

John 1:1-18, 3:16-21; Colossians 1:12-20; Revelation 1:10-18; John 14:6; Acts 4:12; Philippians 2:5-11.

Isaiah 7:14; Matthew 1:18-25; John 1:29-30; Hebrews 10:1-10; 2 Corinthians 5:14-21; Romans 3:21-26, 5:6-11, 8:1-4; Hebrews 10:19-22; 1 John 4:2-4; 2 Peter 3:18; 2 Timothy 1:8-12; Galatians 2:16-20.

Matthew 28:1-20; Luke 24:1-53; Ephesians 1:19-23; Acts 1:4-11; Hebrews 7:24-25.

"A Thinking Man's Filter"

In his classic allegory, *The Holy War*, John Bunyan pictures the intense conflict between Christ and Satan for the possession of the human soul.

When Satan takes Mansoul (the city representative of you or me), that dragon assigns an aide to Mr.

218

Understanding, whose castle of spiritual perception has been shadowed by a tower Satan erected to block its windows.

"To compensate for the darkness imposed upon you, I will give you help," promises the Liar. Satan introduces this helpful aide: His name is *Mr. Mind.*

It is clear that Bunyan, the mightiest penman of his era in church history, whose *Pilgrim's Progress* has stirred, shaped, and stabilized millions in the faith, distrusted the mind of man.

Make no mistake. John Bunyan was no anti-reason, anti-intellect, anti-learning bigot. Neither am I. But like Bunyan, I distrust the human mind. I'm not challenging its sincerity of intent, its brilliant potential, or its marvelous functioning.

I simply distrust its capacity to save us.

Pool the resources of earth's intelligentsia, if you will, but you won't generate salvation. You won't produce a savior.

Many in high circles seem increasingly certain that *information* and its high-tech, strategic availability holds the key to the race's survival—and possibly its glorious success. It is this unsound supposition, so confidently asserted by earth's brain-trustees, that brings us closer and closer to "salvation" by one mega-computer. (I have a hard time looking at those stripes and numbers on my cereal boxes and soup cans and not believing that 666 is hovering just beyond the horizon.)

The authentic Savior—Jesus Christ, Son of God and Lord of Glory—controverted all human preconceptions about messianic deliverance when He surrendered to death on a Roman cross. The result? Resurrection possibilities for all mankind! Life eternal! It was a plan that never would have been devised by the human mind or carried out by human reason (see 1 Corinthians 1:18-25).

God's great salvation plans—indeed, His personal dealings with each of us—force us away from vain trust in even the finest concoctions of our cranium. *"My thoughts are not your thoughts,"* He insists. And that insistence that our minds' analyses will never penetrate to the ultimate answer is an insult to all but the *real* thinking man or woman. The truly enlightened individual learns, however slowly, that our upside-down world-minded patterns can only be set right side up by a different sort of perception.

Years ago, one cigarette company coined a phrase lauding the merits of its filter-tip. This scientifically produced wonder was guaranteed to produce pleasure, and any thinking person would seize this cylinder and puff his or her way to paradise. While rejecting the product, I want to take their phrase and offer you *the* "thinking man's filter."

It's a human spirit breathed to life by the Holy Spirit of God.

Place Him between your mind and your actions. Filter what you think through His purifying, life-producing wisdom before you do anything.

Who knows? You may become an instrument of salvation to a person, a family, a circumstance, a business . . . a city . . . or, dare we believe it? . . . a nation.

You don't *think* so?

Then run that idea through your spirit, and let the Holy Spirit touch it with life. He'll help your heart believe it and quench the futile murmurings of your gray matter.

Don't let Mr. Mind have the last word.

"Listen for The Whispers"

It was the beloved Esther Kerr Rusthoi who coined that phrase, minting it in my consciousness in a priceless way several years ago. It was her way of exhorting believers to "hear what the Holy Spirit is saying to the Church"—or more specifically . . . to you.

To those who refuse to acknowledge a personal God, the suggestion that a loving Father speaks to His children is mocked as mere fantasy. To those ignorant of the Lord Jesus' constant ministry as Head of the Body of His Church, directing the activity of the members of that Body, such communication is considered unnecessary. To those who resist the tender voice of the Holy Spirit's prompting, impressing, balancing, and prodding forward, such "whispers" are labeled fanaticism.

Eli's counsel to young Samuel is still practical wisdom to those who are just beginning to learn to hear the voice of God: "Say, 'Speak, LORD, for Your servant hears'" (1 Samuel 3:9).

Isaiah's prophecy forecasts a way of fruitfulness born from obedience: "Your ears shall hear a word behind you, saying, 'This is the way, walk in it'" (Isaiah 30:21).

Jesus not only taught that sheep will know the Shepherd's voice, but He declared, "My sheep hear My voice . . . and they follow Me." He asserted that receiving His Word—responding to it—is every bit as essential as recognizing it.

Majesty; Jesu

The kind of listening each of these describes is that which brings appropriate action. It is the simple and trusting response of a child, as in Samuel's case, or the sensitive and discerning response of a maturing learner which Isaiah speaks about.

In describing the shepherd/sheep relationship as the basis for this order of hearing, He is saying: (1) If you don't listen, you won't know where He's going, and (2) If you don't respond, you won't be very close to where He is.

In other words, everything is at stake: His guidance and His glory. Without listening carefully, we can miss both.

Friends, I hear a voice.

I think you do, too.

It sometimes calls, sometimes corrects, sometimes commands, sometimes directs, sometimes enthralls, sometimes teaches, sometimes demands, and sometimes reaches . . .

. . . to touch the ear again with a loving, "Follow Me."

Listen.

What is "Being Spiritual"?

Among the funniest things I've ever seen is someone trying to "be spiritual."

You've probably seen it, too.

I'm not talking about hypocrisy—the phony front that seeks to cover insincerity. No, I'm referring to the labored efforts of some sincere people who mean to serve Jesus with all their hearts, but feel obligated to communicate some special aura of "godliness."

The attempt shows up in several ways: an affected tone of voice; a glazed look to the eyes; a certain posture of the head that appears to be trying to balance a halo; a . . . well, just an altogether unnatural bearing that tends to become at least humorous, and at worst, spooky.

Nevertheless, there is a recovery in progress today . . . a recovery of *true spirituality*. It is being experienced in people who are learning that true sanctification is letting the Holy Spirit make you the true you. That doesn't mean you don't need to be transformed—regenerated—born again. You do! Jesus said so in John 3:3,5. Second Corinthians 5:17 makes it clear that the true you *is* a new you.

But that "new" is neither "gooey godly" or "pious prude." When the touch of Jesus comes on a person, He sets in motion the redemption program—that is, His "bringing back from what wasn't" into the "realizing of what was supposed to be."

That's His plan in "redeeming" . . . to take each individual trait in each person's created uniqueness and recover anything that's been lost—erased by sin or failure. God's purpose for each of His beloved sons and daughters is regained. Redemption buys back God's best, after human failure has worked its worst.

This isn't something you strive to accomplish, but it is something you have to want—to open up to—to permit the glory of God's grace to achieve *in* you.

The elements of "being spiritual" have been listed for ages in every kind of disciplinary guide ever formulated or published for believers. These include prayer, Bible reading, fellowship with believers, self-denial, growth in the things of the Holy Spirit, selfless giving, and serving others.

True spirituality, however, somehow just *happens*. Like fruit on a tree. Like flowers on a plant. Like grapes on a vine . . . that's it. Grapes on a vine.

Abide in Me, and I in you. As the branch cannot bear fruit of itself, unless it abides in the vine, neither can you, unless you abide in Me. I am the vine, you are the branches. He who abides in Me, and I in him, bears much fruit; for without Me you can do nothing (John 15:4-5).

Jesus says, "If you abide in Me . . ." it will all begin to happen. Association—a constant link—with Him will produce dissociation—a consuming break—with everything in us that isn't of Him. And when He makes us what God the Father designed us to be, we are relieved of the task of trying to appear as something we *thought* we ought to be.

I've never seen a grape with a hernia . . . or with a halo, for that matter. They neither grunt nor glow . . . they just grow.

That's what "being spiritual" is all about.

With My Eyes Wide Open, I'm Dreaming

That's an old song title, which several of you may remember with me . . . along with a lingering touch of nostalgia.

I'm experiencing something like that these days.

The dream, however, isn't "dreamy." It's real.

I'm not living in an imaginary world. Just invisible.

Joel's prophecy said, "Your old men shall dream dreams." Maybe that means I'm over the hill.

Because I keep dreaming a dream.

I need to define this kind of dreaming, though. Because it isn't the leftover thought processes of a busy yesterday, nor is it the mental machinations resulting from a mushroom and pepperoni pizza tossed into the tummy just before bedtime.

The dream is real. It is God-given. It is, to use a scriptural expression, "seeing the invisible." Any element of "memory" it entails is the remembrance of the fact that our Almighty Father can do anything: *There is nothing too hard for You, Lord.* And insofar as "imagination" is involved, the "image" is something proceeding from His mind and becoming implanted in mine. The idea is His . . . and it is not at all uncommon in the Word that the Lord communicates His will by dreams.

Not mystical dreams. Not fantastic dreams. Not puzzling dreams. Not weird, wonder-what-this-means dreams. But in dreams nonetheless; a vision born in the mind and heart by the Holy Spirit. A vision which becomes so thoroughly possessing of one's thoughts that it is a tangible reality in his or her experience.

And that's the way God works.

He has an idea, determines His will, and then brings it to pass. In teaching us to move after the pattern of His workings, He begins by giving us His idea. We receive it as a dream. His Holy Spirit impresses us with the confirming certainty that this idea is His will. And as soon as an idea from God is known to be the will of God, His Word tells us exactly what to do. Pray: "Your will be done on earth as it is in heaven."

From that time on, what you know He sees as an

already-accomplished fact begins more and more to appear to you in the same condition. Done. A dream come true. And praise begins to follow on the heels of prayer.

What do you see the Father willing for your life? Let it happen. Receive the dream, and possess it in prayer as you call on Him in Jesus' wonderful name. This isn't so much "positive thought" or "self-persuasion" baloney. It is simply a biblical pathway to receiving God's intended purpose for a group of His people . . . or for you, His deeply loved child.

Dream on!

I've Never Taken It Away

I woke.
Another day of pain, I thought.
The aching doubts, constraining fears,
The dark assaults.
Declining years, I thought,
So this is what it's like.

I rolled in bed.
Come now, get up, I thought.
And kneeling there beside my cot
      breathed out my fears;
Expressed my prayer,
O Father, once again, I cried,
Please place Your hand upon my life.

And in the darkness by my bed,
    He spoke,
    The word was quick,
        and crystal clear:
"I've never taken it away;
I'm here to bless another year,
My touch upon you e'er will stay—
It's firm—for all your life, your days.
I've *never* taken it away."

He's never taken it away!
    Dear God,
That word dissolves the fears.
Your mighty hand will always stay;
    O, how that word now
        draws me near:
    To walk with patience,
        portage tears,
        or press the battle.
For it's clear,
    He's here and here He'll always be,
    For all my life—eternally!
His hand is on you,
    Soul, give praise!
He's never taken it away.[12]

glory, honor, and

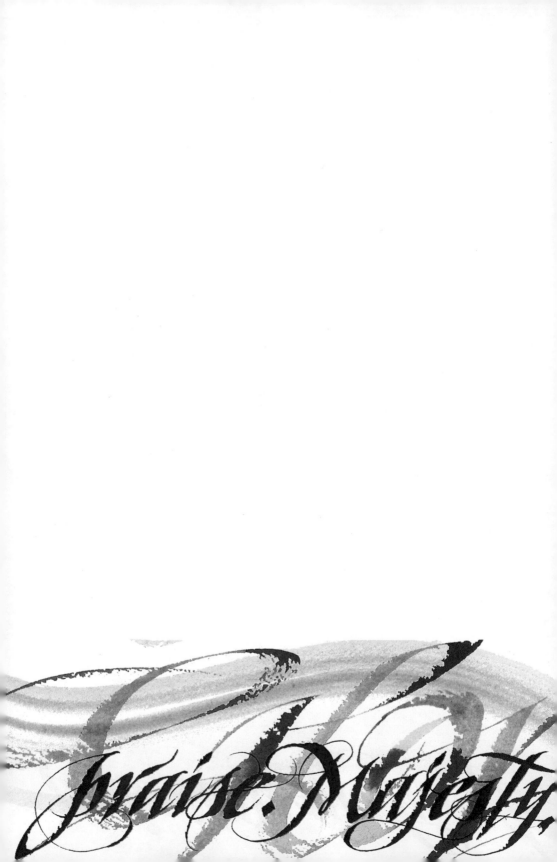

praise Majesty,

NOVEMBER

Thanksgiving

kingdom authority-

Glory and honor,
praise and thanksgiving,
to Jesus the Lord of Lords,
the Lamb who was slain.

flow from His

Cycles

The trees along my walking route splashed their spectrum of color against the November sky. A surge of emotion rose within me. With a thankful heart and tear-filled eyes, I prayed . . .

Father, I thank You for letting me enjoy this beauty, and for helping me to rejoice in it all the more . . .

. . . because I know YOU, the Creator of it all,

. . . because I understand how MUCH You delight in creating such magnificence for our enjoyment,

. . . because I KNOW Your nature is to bless and benefit each of us, Your creatures,

. . . because You've SHOWN by these seasonal means the constancy of Your own being—towering beyond time, but stooping to touch us within it.

And as I take this walk, dear Lord, I praise You that I, like the seasons themselves, have tasted Your restoring cycle of sustaining power . . . even in my own body.

It was very moving to me, for since a back injury almost a year before, I had not been able to take the frequent strolls I had so enjoyed. Now I was beginning to resume the former pattern, and I was *deeply* thankful.

Only a few days earlier I had ventured out for an attempt at the kind of walk I used to take—the length and the pace—and returned home with special happiness that "I had made it." Walking into the kitchen, I said to Anna, "You know, Honey, that's the first time I've been able to take 'my walk,' and when I turned the corner just now, the Lord brought something to my mind. It's exactly one year ago today that I hurt my back! It was as though He was saying, 'The cycle of trial is behind you; the cycle of restoration is beginning.'"

Her eyes misted like mine as I said, "I really believe the Lord is going to make me completely well—all the way!"

Now I was on my fourth outing, and doing well. And with the faith, hope, and joy that was crowding into corners of my soul which I didn't realize had been so cob-webbed with uncertainty, a song began to rise:

> As I look up to the heavens and my eye scans the oceans,
> I am filled with emotions inexpressible. . . .

But rather than finish that song right now, this Thanksgiving season I want to invite you to take a walk *with* me, though perhaps not "at my side." Take a stroll someday soon, and let your *heart* study the Creator's grand workings which surround you.

Look at the leaves. Listen to the wind. Study the stars. As you do, remember this: The Almighty One of creative power is the All-Loving One of grace. Whatever your present need, trial, or struggle might be, He is the One who governs cycles and seasons.

His hand governs the seasons of the year. His love guides the seasons of your life.

A Peculiar and Then a Precious Thanksgiving

It was our first Thanksgiving in the pastorate, and I was savoring my first taste of autumn in the Midwest.

Anna and I were living in the land of James Whitcomb Riley, who wrote, "When the frost is on the punkin and the fodder's in the shock." His writings had stirred my esthetic gastric juices since my teen-age years, and now I was seeing it—Indian summer in Indiana . . . flaming trees, singing winds, frosty designs on the windowpane, leaves scurrying before you and then crunching under your feet.

Anna was pregnant with our first baby, and the only family within a thousand miles was our tiny congregation. How heartwarmed we were when one of the couples invited us to their house for the holiday dinner.

And then . . .

I hardly know how to describe the disappointment. It was immediately clear that the dear people who had asked us over had no sense of proportion or appreciation for Thanksgiving. There was nothing—absolutely nothing—special about the day, the meal, the atmosphere, the conversation. It wasn't that they lacked resources, they simply lacked perspective and social grace.

Mind you, Anna and I were neither critical nor inappreciative. We were bewildered, chagrined—and so deeply disappointed.

We drove home about 5:00 P.M. in the gathering

darkness. Quiet. Puzzled. The three preceding hours of dinner and talk were not bad—they simply weren't "Thanksgiving." We rode along in silence, *trying* to be grateful for what we had received. I slipped my arm around Anna. Sensing and sharing my disappointment, she said, "What a strange Thanksgiving."

Neither of us felt pitiful, but I doubt it would have taken much to induce tears.

And then, again.

The phone rang. It was 6:30 the same evening. One of the older couples in the church was on the line. "Jack . . . Anna, we're just getting ready to make some turkey sandwiches and have some more stuffing, sweet potatoes, cranberries, and all. Could you come over for a snack?"

Could we?! Wow! They only lived two blocks from our house, and I think we arrived as he was hanging up the phone.

The conversation was as good as the food, because, you see, Bob and Margaret had just received Jesus a few weeks before. Thanksgiving meant more than ever to them. And to Anna and me, too. It was precious . . . and still is.

Since then, I always want to help others toward a treasured Thanksgiving. Will you join me in ministering through this holiday season to people? Look around. There are young Jacks and Annas and Bobs and Margarets everywhere around you—lonely and longing for a touch of home . . . for a touch of Jesus' love.

Let's be the family we're meant to be.

lift up on high

Biblical "Plenties"

While in Bristol, England, a few years ago, I found this list of biblical "plenties." Use it for a reminder to *count* your blessings, and use it as a prompter from His promises to *expect* His blessings.

Plenty of Food: "You shall eat in plenty and be satisfied" (Joel 2:26).

Plenty of Water: "You, O God, sent a plentiful rain" (Psalm 68:9).

Plenty of Goods: "The LORD will grant you plenty of goods" (Deuteronomy 28:11).

Plenty of Production: "The LORD your God will make you abound in all the work of your hand . . . " (Deuteronomy 30:9).

Plenty in Store: "So your barns will be filled with plenty" (Proverbs 3:10); " . . . bread enough and to spare" (Luke 15:17).

Plenty for All: " . . . A bountiful country" (Jeremiah 2:7).

Plenty of Mercy: "Slow to anger, and plenteous in mercy" (Psalm 103:8, KJV).

Plentiful Pardon: "Return to the LORD . . . for He will abundantly pardon" (Isaiah 55:7).

Plentiful Peace: "And the peace of God, which surpasses all understanding, will guard your hearts and minds through Christ Jesus" (Philippians 4:7).

Plentiful Redemption: "With the Lord there is mercy, and with Him is abundant redemption" (Psalm 130:7); "For God so loved the world that He gave His only begotten Son, that whoever believes in Him should not perish but have everlasting life" (John 3:16).

Plentiful Grace: "And God is able to make all grace abound toward you, that you, always having all sufficiency in all things, have an abundance for every good work" (2 Corinthians 9:8).

Plentiful Resources: "Now to Him who is able to do exceedingly abundantly above all that we ask or think, according to the power that works in us" (Ephesians 3:20).

Plenty for the Future: "Eye has not seen, nor ear heard, nor have entered into the heart of man the things which God has prepared for those who love Him" (1 Corinthians 2:9).

God makes no apology for *willing* to lavish life's fullness on us, over us, and around us. "Life more abundantly" is still the divine intent. Go ahead. Slide up to your Father's table and help yourself.

Heavenly Father, I Appreciate...

You, first, my Father.

I bow, overwhelmed by abundance of mercy, grace, and glory which You have so profusely lavished upon me and all that concerns me.

I appreciate the changeless things which surround my life . . .

Magnify, come

. . . the security in the blood of the everlasting
covenant;
. . . the presence of Jesus, Your love-gift Son;
. . . the fullness of Your gift-giving Spirit;
For changeless things, I appreciate You, Father.

I appreciate changing things . . .
. . . painted sunsets, never duplicated;
. . . colored leaves splashing on my street as this season changes;
. . . the gray hair tinging my own temples;
. . . the eternal prospect of a new body when this
one wears out;
For new clothes, new books, new days, and for mercies
that are new every morning . . . I appreciate You.

And how I appreciate the immense gifts you have
given me packaged in *people*. For the precious members
and friends of the flock that surround this shepherd, for
the fellow pastors who make the tending of these beloved
ones possible, for innumerable volunteers who give themselves tirelessly while increasing numbers of those they
serve open their hearts to the eternal gift of life in Your
Son. Thank You, Abba God.

I am crushed with the kindness You have shown me
in my family, and that crushing exudes a fragrance of
praise rising from the pressure of such beauty abounding
upon me. Thank You for my children, who are pursuing
Your direction in their lives. Thank You for my grandchil-
dren—just two, so far—one in our arms and one being
formed even now in the womb, but alive already with
eternal capacities.

And for Anna . . . I weep with thanksgiving—that
You have graced me with a gracious and lovely woman
who shares my joys, sorrow, trials, and triumphs with
patience, understanding, tenderness, and strength as my
partner in life.

238

While lifting my hands in appreciation to You, Father, I pray: *Let the Spirit of praiseful appreciation abound in the midst of the flock you have privileged me to feed as their pastor. For these . . . and all who read these words, I pray that You would enrich them all with the same joy which floods my soul.*

And, by the way, Father, I appreciate that You have caused them to love and appreciate me.

For such miracles, I praise You!

The Song of Harvest Home

It is not commonly known that the Pilgrims' original Thanksgiving celebration was not their first such experience. All of them had been raised in a culture which observed a similar time of praise each harvesttime.

"Harvest home" was the name of a feast celebrated in England (and in some places still is today) when the last of the harvest was brought in. The words "harvest home" were obviously coined in the announcement that "All the harvest is now home. It's all gathered, in the barn, and we're ready for winter to come!"

Henry Alford's hymn, "Come, Ye Thankful People," written well over a century ago, was designed to lead his congregation in praise on a day of thanksgiving. His sobering lyric not only observes the gratitude we owe to God, but the accountability which ought to occur to our hearts when such bounty is gathered.

God has blessed us, though He owes us *nothing*.

We should praise and serve Him faithfully, for we
owe Him *everything*.

Come, ye thankful people, come,
Raise the song of harvest-home:
All is safely gathered in
Ere the winter storms begin.
God, our Maker, doth provide
For our wants to be supplied:
Come to God's own temple, come,
Raise the song of harvest-home.

All the world is God's own field,
Fruit unto His praise to yield:
Wheat and tares together sown,
Unto joy or sorrow grown;
First the blade and then the ear,
Then the full corn shall appear:
Lord of harvest, grant that we
Wholesome grain and pure may be.

For the Lord our God shall come
And shall take His harvest home:
From His field shall in that day
All offenses purge away;
Give His angels charge at last
In the fire the tares to cast,
But the fruitful ears to store
In His garner evermore.[13]

Alford's hymn draws an analogy between the gathered harvest of each autumn and the final harvest of
mankind. Jesus, in Matthew 13, described the Ultimate
Harvest as the gathering of all human souls to be brought
before God. The sensitive soul will be reminded of the
separation of the wheat and the tares—the redeemed and
the unsaved. This Thanksgiving season, let none of us
take lightly the goodness which provides salvation. We

can *all* plan on an eternal feast of thanks by simply receiving the bounty of forgiveness and love the Father God offers us in His Son Jesus.

"For God so loved the world, He gave His Son. . . ." That Son allowed Himself to be sown as a seed buried in death, that the great harvest of our souls might be gathered unto eternal life.

Let's lift our voices, saints! On this day—and every day—we are:

People who are blessed by the *abundance* of God's hand;

People who have received *love and grace* beyond measure;

People redeemed to *eternal life* through Jesus Christ our Lord;

People granted the *peace and privilege* of celebration in a land blessed far beyond anything we deserve;

People allowed a day to *focus* on thanks and *feast* with freedom; and . . .

People *destined to an eternal feast* of high joy forever.

Let's sing with Henry Alford:

Even so, Lord, quickly come
To Thy final harvest home:
Gather Thou Thy people in,
Free from sorrow, free from sin;
There, forever purified,
In Thy presence to abide:
Come, with all Thine angels, come,
Raise the glorious harvest-home.[14]

All This Splendor

En route to the airport to meet someone recently, the seasonal beauty around me evoked a sudden surge of joy. It found expression on my lips in a phrase: *"All this splendor, God, surrounds me . . ."*

I took a pen from my pocket and began to scribble on a note pad on the seat beside me. Each red traffic light provided time to write the next phrase. While it wasn't until after meeting the plane—in fact, not until the next day—that I finished, the following resulted from that experience of season-change-time joyfulness. If you're musically inclined, the lyrics of the poem may be sung as a hymn to the melody of Beethoven's "Joyful, Joyful, We Adore Thee."

All this splendor, God, surrounds me,
    I cannot contain it all.
Gifts abound by your hand given,
    Seen in great things and in small.
Tow'ring mountains rise to witness
    Of my great Creator's skill,
While a baby's touch is speaking
    Of my loving Father's will.

Autumn leaves and winter snowdrifts,
    Springtime green and summer gold;
Each in turn gives testimony
    Of the Mighty Hand I hold.
His the touch that brings the seasons;
    His the finger moves the wind.

That same hand once pierced by treason
    Now enfolds me though I've sinned.
Splendid, O my God, Your workings,
    How my heart o'erflows today.
Your creation and redemption
    Stand as wonders—theme my praise.
Lord, receive this creature's worship;
    Hear this thankful son's new song.
Yours the power, mine the praises;
    Ours the joy all ages long.[15]

Join me in giving high and special praise to our blessed Lord God, the Creator of earth's beauty. The din and the smog of city-dwelling can dull our senses to the magnificence He shines toward us—especially at season-changes.

Rejoice with me, and while noting the *grandeur* of His creative working, take comfort in the *personal* and *tender* reach of His hand toward you.

Keepers
of
The Flame

The memory came back to me just recently. Now that I think about it, it seems remarkable. But when I was growing up, it didn't seem remarkable at all.

Every time I ever saw my daddy take a drink of water, he paused to thank the Lord. He would fill a glass and then say, "I want to thank You for this water, in Jesus' Name, Amen."

glorified King

Daddy was one who took 1 Thessalonians 5:18 very literally.

In everything give thanks; for this is the will of God in Christ Jesus for you.

Over the years, I have become convinced that praise sets up a mantle of protection around the people of the Lord. Praise is an atmosphere through which the Adversary cannot move.

If you and I really entered into this truth, it would transform our lives. And it's not simply because praise can insulate or protect us. It's more than that. It is because *He is worthy* . . . worthy of the best of our praise, the depths of our thanksgiving. As you ask the Lord to teach you more and more about the tireless, ongoing spirit of praise, it will change your character, it will change your circumstances, it will change your countenance.

In the Old Testament, the Lord gave instructions to Moses about the "perpetual fire" that was to burn on the altar inside the Tent of Meeting.

Command Aaron and his sons, saying, "This is the law of the burnt offering: The burnt offering shall be on the hearth upon the altar all night until morning, and the fire of the altar shall be kept burning on it (Leviticus 6:9).

The Lord went on to describe several matters about the changing of priestly clothes and the disposal of the ashes, concluding with this final reminder:

A perpetual fire shall burn on the altar; it shall never go out (Leviticus 6:13).

The Lord was telling His priests, you're going to be doing your job day in and day out, and there will be all kinds of different things going on, such as changing your clothes and dumping ashes. But in the midst of it all, *keep the flame burning. Never let it go out.*

The writer of Hebrews describes the only remaining sacrifice for New Testament believers when he states:

Therefore by Him [Jesus] let us continually offer the sacrifice of praise to God, that is, the fruit of our lips, giving thanks to His name (13:15).

Notice the word *continually*. Keep the flame of praise burning in your life continually. Ceaselessly. In all circumstances. Now this doesn't mean we become some kind of recluse from society. I'm not suggesting that you get in some private cubicle in a monastic corner of the universe where you repeat formula praises every waking hour.

I think the Lord is simply saying, "Whatever you do, whether you're changing your clothes or taking out the trash or driving along the freeway, just keep the flame burning. Be a praiser. Keep in an attitude of praise. Never let the flame die out. Never let the fire be quenched."

When you think about the glory-worthiness of Jesus Christ, such glory-glowing doesn't seem too much to ask.

Light up. And keep burning.

Somewhere To Go

My daddy went home last Thursday afternoon. Through the mercy of God he was relieved of extensive suffering, and by the grace of God is at home with Christ Jesus, his and our Savior and Lord.

Through my frequent references to him in sermon anecdotes, my flock at The Church On The Way have come to know him and his place in shaping my understanding of the heavenly Father. Those facts, coupled with his and Mama's occasional holiday visits here, have familiarized and endeared them to many. In a way perhaps unknowable to any of us, he will be missed by this congregation, for nobody prayed more than him for me and my flock.

A rush of tender memories come to mind, and during the ten days leading up to his homegoing, I was able to share many of them with him in conversation.

My father—we always called him "Daddy"—is a classic case study of greatness without renown; of spiritual strength mixed with lovable human weaknesses. He was a pillar among the people of God and an elder who ministered to the Body of Christ wherever the Holy Spirit directed him.

The Saturday morning before Daddy left, the Lord impressed me deeply with a truth I already knew—but had not seen so preciously before. It is the fact of our having the certainty of a specific place to go when our life-work here is ended. I was thinking about Daddy's impending departure to "go home," and suddenly felt the joy in the sense of our having a *personal destination*.

Heaven is a blessed hope, and Jesus' personal presence a magnificent expectation, but His own words struck me: "I go to prepare *a place for you*" (John 14:2). Christ's salvation is *so* complete, including a promise of an eternal place to go.

No drifting. No wandering souls wafting in the ether. Heaven is not ethereal, but we will be with Jesus in person and in the personal place He's made for each of us.

Daddy's home now, after a sixty-six year journey here. He was a man of God, a saint, made holy through the work of Christ's Cross, and ready to stand before God in the robes of righteousness He provides.

Yes, Daddy was "all dressed up."   And, praise God, he had somewhere to go.

A Gift of Thanksgiving

Ah, Lord, we bring praise and honor
    As a gift of thanksgiving to You.
For Your great grace and Your strong
        loving-kindness
Now invite our gratitude anew.

So Lord, we come empty-handed,
    Lifting only our hearts with our voices;
Now we sing to express gratitude with humbleness
For the way You provide, ever guide, and always bless.

    We give thanks for the way
    You delight to delight us each day.

Ah, Lord, every tree and mountain
    Rises up with a witness to You.
Fruitful fields speak of Your unchanging
        goodness,
And your mercy sparkles in the dew.

Wind, rain, falling leaves of autumn,
    Winter snow, springing flow'rs, and the sun shine
Forth the light of Your love; countless blessings from above,
As from season to season in You we live and move—

Unto Jesus he

Moved to praise You alway
For the brightness You pour on our way.

Great God, as a gifted nation
We have tasted Your bounty and grace.
So we bow now with this gift of thanksgiving
To present our worship and our praise.

Dear God, hear our prayer for mercy
As our song of thanksgiving we raise, pray
Now forgive us, O Lord. Lead us forward by Your Word.
By the pow'r of Your hand, spread Your grace across our
land,

That we ever may be
Thankful people of praise unto thee.[16]

praise Majesty

DECEMBER

Wonder

...kingdom authority...

That You came is a wonder to me.
That You came changed all history.
That You came changed my destiny.

flow from His

The Inescapable Christ

His life is the light that shines through the darkness—and the darkness can never extinguish it (John 1:5, TLB).

It was the day after Thanksgiving, and everything you might imagine the word "throngs" to represent surrounded us. Anna and I were caught up and borne along by the crowds of Christmas shoppers on Fifth Avenue and then Madison Avenue in New York City.

We had brunch in a Central Park restaurant and visited Saks to behold the decorations. We stopped to listen to a Salvation Army ensemble honor Jesus, then peeled and munched warm chestnuts which had literally been "roasting on an open fire." From there it was on to Bloomingdale's and Macy's.

It was in Bloomingdale's—one of America's most famous department stores—that it struck me again.

"Hark, the herald angels sing, glory to the newborn King," the P.A. system sang forth. We strolled past a display of wood carvings next to another one of miniskirts.

"Jesus, Lord, at Thy birth," the closing words of "Silent Night" declared, *"Jesus, Lord, at Thy birth."*

The strains of Handel's "Hallelujah Chorus" wafted

through the toy department. Then, as we surveyed the Christmas ornament display, yet another carol echoed from the walls.

I felt deeply moved. "Strange, isn't it?" I mused to Anna. "This metropolis—so captivated by its own secularism and sophistication—can't get away from Him."

Jesus is the central personality of history, and whether Christmas is canned or canonized, packaged in ribbon and sold for profit or sanctified in a cathedral where humble souls worship, He is the inescapable Christ. The fury of demon-inspired opposition to His praise seeks to ban pageantry and sterilize holy celebration to suit the antagonism of organized unbelief.

But Jesus keeps rising again.

Every Christmas turns out to be an Easter. The irrepressible power of His life keeps the song rolling from age to age. It was all overwhelming to me as I listened to each melody and savored the witness of their lyrics.

Anna paused at a counter and I wandered over to a chair and sat down. As I did, the following sprang to mind, perfectly fitted to the beloved Welsh melody, Ashgrove.

Lord Jesus our Savior,
The Gift of the Father's favor
Appeared in a lowly manger,
    On this Christmas Day.

With carols loudly ringing,
And bright voices gladly singing,
Our praise joyously we're bringing,
    On this Christmas Day.

There is naught ever to compare with the
Love He has come to share with us;
God come as man to bear with us
    All of our need.

And thus the revelation of
God's gracious salvation
Which themes all our celebration
    On this Christmas Day.[17]

It was a special post-Thanksgiving, pre-Christmas event, getting to enjoy the season's opening in one of our nation's largest cities. But what I liked most was the discovery of just one more piece of evidence . . .

Jesus Christ is still the King of kings.

Unwrapping Christmas

Christmas month begins. And again I find myself wanting to reach out to help people who can't, by themselves, "unwrap" Christmas. It is, you know, "wrapped" for many . . .

> . . . wrapped in the bandages of bygone hurts and disappointments,
>
> . . . wrapped in the plastic of sophistication which prohibits childlike wonder,
>
> . . . wrapped in the tinsel of a materialistic binge,
>
> . . . wrapped in the confetti and streamers of empty partying,
>
> . . . wrapped in the busy-getting-ready preparations,
>
> . . . wrapped in the artistically designed whiskey box of bombed-out, so-called "celebrations."

The Ghost of Christmas Past returns to haunt numberless now-redeemed members of the Father's forever-family, but without the beneficial results produced by Scrooge's specter.

The "wrappings" listed are not necessarily reflective of one's current hindrance, but rather, the cluttered residue of a person's private history. They are the wadded packagings of Christmases ruined in other times, at other places. Sadly, the impact carries on, souring year after year. I'm speaking of people . . .

- who had a heartbreak one Yuletide, and now always associate the season with that tearful memory,

- who have been burned out over family stresses surrounding the holidays, so that now these days are dreaded instead of anticipated with joy,

- who became wearied with the carnality of superficial gift giving when love seldom attended the presents, and now wince at the idea of Christmas shopping.

How many cases? How many varieties of death wrap a God-appointed celebration of *life*?

I come to you, today, friend, in Jesus' Name. Confronting those ghouls of past pain, I pray with you: "Father, forgive us our Christmases, as we forgive those who Christmased against us." And I say, "Be free, dear one!"

Through Jesus—the Babe become King, the Son become Lord, the Child become Christ—in His mighty Name, lay hold of this festal day with rejoicings. Refuse to let the Prince of Darkness smother the Season of Light. The one who sought to murder the Baby of Bethlehem now seeks to ruin your celebration of His coming. Resist him with all the strength Your Lord provides.

Be untied. Be unfettered. Be unwrapped. Take my hands, and together . . .

Let's dance toward Christmas!

lift up on high

Visions of Sugar Plums

A fire danced and crackled in the fireplace, our Advent candle flickered in the soft light, and the mellow voice of Nat King Cole wafted through the living room. We sat there . . . together.

Together as at all times of the year, yet together as at no other time of the year. Our family. Not all of us at that particular moment that one evening, but all together anyway. Maybe just Anna and me along with half our offspring, Jack and Christy. Mark? He's down the street baby-sitting at a neighbor's. Becki? She's married now, beginning a Christmas tradition of her own.

But even with the scattering, we are together. Not just at Christmas . . . and yet, somehow, especially at Christmas.

Nostalgia, sentimentalism, seasonal emotion—none of the terms answer to this sense of fulfillment that fills me at this season. The finest quality of human love, the highest dimension of family devotion—neither adequately account for it. You can attempt to give an intellectual analysis of my psychological state or simply write off my condition as some adult stage of "visions of sugar plums."

But that won't do either. There is only one way to account for this.

Jesus lives at our house.

And it's His birthday.

His presence is real, and the preciousness with which the Holy Spirit communicates deep dimensions of His love among us when His annual incarnational celebration recurs is absolutely joyous. He is the Spirit of Christmas—holy is His name. And whether you are thinking of the *Baby* in the manger, the *Child* whose parents escaped with Him into Egypt, the *Teenager* in the temple in Jerusalem, the *Prophet* scattering moneychangers' tables, the *Healer* restoring vision to blind eyes, the *Deliverer* liberating the demoniac, the *Teacher* revealing the truth of the eternal Father, the *Savior* dying upon Calvary, the *Lord* rising from the dead, or *Christ His Majesty* ruling on high at the Father's right hand . . . He's here this Christmas. The Holy Spirit makes that very real.

You don't need candlelight and fireside glow to make it happen. Trees, ornaments, gifts, and all of it are splendid embellishments. Not necessary, but so very nice.

It's *Him*. He's finding more and more opened inns these days. It's priceless to discover the pleasure of His company, and especially when He's in a celebrating mood.

May your home know something of all this glory during these days. It's no sugar-plum vision. We've found the real thing.

I Can't Imagine The Eternal Mon

. . . When the Father rose from the throne, turned to the Son, and said, "Now."

What exchange of words accompanied the laying

Magnify, come

aside of His robes of glory? As He humbly divested Himself of every rank His due, each power His own, what thoughts traversed His mind?

"A body You have prepared for Me," speaks the Son trustingly. "Behold, I have come—in the volume of the book it is written of Me" (Hebrews 10:5,7).

Did an angel entourage accompany Him to the gates of the eternal city? At His departure, what bewilderment appeared upon angelic countenances, since they were not privy to the in-workings of the eternal plan? (1 Peter 1:12)

What pain did the Father feel? He alone knew the depths to which these processes would take His Son. He alone foresaw the impact of human sin and ignorance, and with what destructive force it would break over the head of His Only-Begotten.

What silence this hour, for the Son's exit is not Christmas Eve. The song of angels shall be withheld for thousands of earth hours yet to be, for presently He leaves not for a manger in Bethlehem, but for a womb in Nazareth.

God, a fetus. The most incredible concept of all. How? What wonder is this? Miracles and a resurrection are easy to believe once this truth is received: "The Word became flesh and dwelt among us" (John 1:14). Confidence in heaven's concern with earth's need is certain when we lay hold of the words, "Since we, God's children, are human beings—made of flesh and blood—he became flesh and blood too by being born in human form" (Hebrews 2:14, TLB).

God, a baby!

The ultimate vulnerability: God surrendering Himself to man. It extends beyond the limits of human imagination, but not beyond human comprehension. Because of the unimaginable I can experience the comprehensible. Because of the eternal expenditure that the Father made—giving His Beloved—and because of the redemptive price the Son would pay—giving His blood—I can be born again. Forgiven. Transformed. Brought to the Father forever.

It is all finally comprehensible because it can happen in me. But it somehow remains unimaginable when I attempt to conceive how His conception came about. But it did. And because of that morn, I awaken on this one to greet you.

The Magic of Christmas

In a period when satanic operations and methods are increasing and becoming more apparent, many of us, myself included, have withdrawn from the use of certain words.

The word "magic" is an example. Because of its relationship to superstition and deceptions, as well as to the realm of black arts and evil supernaturalism, one hesitates to use it. It seems its age of innocence is gone.

But C. S. Lewis redeemed the word "magic" for me in his book, *The Lion, the Witch, and the Wardrobe*. He qualifies and distinguishes the evil from the good by the use of the adjective "deeper." The land of Narnia may lie under a curse as a result of the White Witch's magic, but the "deeper magic," worked through the lion Aslan's death, breaks the curse.

Christmas is a "deeper magic."

Beyond the spell of lights, carols, gifts, goodies, ornaments, tinsel, holly, plum pudding, mistletoe, stars, and generally endless loveliness, it's the magic of one specific miracle that captivates me.

"The Word became flesh."

That's the magic—the deeper kind—of this majestic season. Unquestionably, the mightiest magic of all is reflected in those few words from the prologue to the Gospel of John. God entered the arena of man. But more than that . . . *He became one.*

God . . . a man.

Please note. That wasn't "Man . . . a god." That image had been destroyed. Every human system of redemption is based on the supposition that man can somehow recover his lost estate by the energy of the flesh. Flesh ceaselessly attempts to re-climb the heights of its lost nobility and destiny. But all that the flesh can ultimately produce in its own strength is sweat. And the odor of the flesh's product is a commentary on its sufficiency.

No, God became flesh. Interesting, isn't it, how that one word "became" not only describes an entrance, but it also suggests a beautification. "The new coat you wore," we say, "became you . . . (or) It was so becoming." God became flesh. Not only in that He "wore it well" (and my, how Jesus did that!) but further—flesh has been eternally enhanced as a result of His taking it on Himself.

Think on that.

Let Christmas in its deepest magic possess your mind. It will alter and stimulate everything about your observance of the special season we now share. The Lord of Glory, "endless, eternal and unchangeable in His being, wisdom, power, and holiness," became man. Became a *baby*. Purpose: That the race which lost paradise might have a second chance at it.

In that moment, the unseen world invaded the tainted

tangible. Purpose: That the untouchable God might be reached unto, and when man would touch Him he would be made whole.

That WORD which became flesh has a name. And approaching this day of days, at this season of seasons, let the splendor of that Man above men sparkle upon your lips.

Jesus.

The Light Has Come

I was flying home several Christmases ago and as my jet descended toward the Burbank airport, my heart leaped within me. The valley floor was a carpet of multi-colored lights woven from a million strands, composed of wire-like cords which string bulbs across rooftops. A hundred thousand window frames were embroidered in color, like ginger-breaded Swiss chalets.

My eyes teared up and I began to sing praises to God the Father . . . to Jesus the Son-given . . . and the Holy Spirit overflowed my mouth with worship. I was caught up in awe at the way God has, with majestic cleverness, "caught" mankind with Christmas. Inescapably, the glory creeps across the landscape worldwide. None can deny it. *The Light has come.*

Man is trapped into testimony. And the lights declare it: *The Light has come.* Suddenly, and for the most part unwittingly, across the face of the earth a billion of mankind rise with light in their hands to testify to it. It may not have even penetrated their hearts or their minds as yet, but with candles, torches, and bulbs they announce the fact: *The Light has come!*

I sat at my desk late the other evening, our family having just finished decorating our tree, and I wrote:

> The Light has come and the darkness can
> Never be the same, O hallelujah!
> The Light has shone and the darkness ran
> Never to return, O hallelu!
> Your Word made flesh, Your Glory revealed;
> Its entrance gave great light.
> You spoke, He came: Christ Jesus His name.
> And He has scattered our night.
> The Light has come and the darkness can
> Never be the same, O hallelujah!
> And now the Light shines to ev'ry man.
> You can live in light, O hallelu!
>
> The sound of joy fills the earth and sky and the bells
> peal forth their hallelujah!
> The day has dawned and the sun climbs high,
> for the Light has come, O hallelu!
> This Child now born, Himself is the truth;
> the Truth which sets men free.
> His glory shines to all of mankind
> and His light brings liberty.
> The sound of joy fills the earth and sky and the bells
> peal forth their hallelujah!
> With freedom's song lift your voice and
> cry, Jesus Christ is Lord, O hallelu!
>
> A silver beam splits the sky above
> and His star appears, O hallelujah!
> A glory stream spreading hope and love
> as Messiah comes, O hallelu!
> He tramples darkness under His feet,
> His battle flag unfurled;
> Despair and bondage shatter and flee,
> for He's the Light of the world.
> A silver beam splits the sky above and His star
> appears, O hallelujah!

His kingdom come is a rule of love,
  casting out all fear, O hallelu!
The Light has come and for ev'ry man
  Life has come to light, O hallelujah!
Tho' some resist it, they never can
  overcome its power, O hallelu!
For God in flesh once walked on the earth
  as Jesus, Son of Man.
The splendor of His glory displayed
  continues ages to span.
The Light has come and to ev'ry man
  Life has come to light, O hallelujah!
And as it shines unto me I can
  Be renewed in life, O hallelu![18]

It's true. The undeniable reality which has ignited your heart and mine is flaming from housetops with an unquenchable message: "In Him was life, and the life was the light of men. And the light shines in the darkness . . . That was the true Light which gives light to every man who comes into the world" (John 1:4,5,9).

As this holy fire leaps higher this season, would you join me in a commitment?

Lord, I will not be satisfied with the wealth of joy and life You have caused to be mine, until I can share it with EVERY ONE. You have lighted the candle of my spirit; I will take it and touch others, until the world is purified by Your consuming flame.

glorified Kin

Living Above Condemnation

For God did not send His Son into the world to condemn the world, but that the world through Him might be saved (John 3:17).

The merriness surrounding Christmas is directly attributable and essentially related to God's gift of Jesus. To us. For us.

The Son of God has come,
light has entered the world,
a Savior is here and
our sins can be forgiven!

Apart from these glorious facts, there is no logic to the season's existence, much less the festive rejoicing which we share.

We celebrate these great facts. Not just at Christmastime but through every day of our journey. The days we are walking through derive their meaning and highest fulfillment from these truths which distill from this grand reality: God is with us!

We rejoice because Joy has come to earth, we give gifts because the grandest One has been given to us, we feast because the Bread of Life has been provided, and we sing carols of endless variety because all of life has been penetrated by The Song.

Still, amid all the brightness, innumerable souls remain shadowed. The power of human failure to stain the soul is immeasurable. Even years after the sin and the failure, the defeat and darkness continue to shade tomorrow's horizons. The impress of guilt leaves ridges in the mind, and in the valleys beneath them shafts of sunlight rarely appear. Condemnation is a dark demon which clouds the soul, stifles hope, and resists any attempt to gain confidence for tomorrow.

As we light our Christmas candles this month, let's ask our mighty Savior to burn out these shadows. Let's lift our praise to the One who came to break the back of condemnation, restore us to union with our Father-Creator, cleanse and purify our souls through His Cross, and fill us with God's Holy Spirit to enable us to become what we were made to be.

In John's Gospel, Jesus explained the one reason condemnation ever has a right to remain in any heart: "This is the condemnation, that the light has come into the world, and men loved darkness rather than light, because their deeds were evil" (3:19).

In short, the only people who need bear condemnation from God are those who prefer their own way to His.

So as we complete this season, join me in a dual declaration:

I receive Your Light, Lord Jesus—purge my soul and let me live in Your Light; and

I will share Your Light—that having so freely received of Your love, I will freely give.

Sing it again:

The Light has come and the darkness can never be the same . . . Hallelujah!

The Testimony of the Tree

The arrangement and decoration of a Christmas tree at our church as a part of our Christmas celebration is a specific statement, not an occasional or accidental surrender to a mere cultural tradition. By means of this tree we are saying:

We believe in celebration.

We serve the God who "gives us richly all things to enjoy" (1 Timothy 6:17), and who through history assigned to His people sacred appointments of feasting and rejoicing. While God is neither a giddy Roman Bacchus nor a frumpy American Santa, He is a "blessed" or "happy" God (1 Timothy 1:11). Through Jesus Christ, He has introduced life into the light. It is in this light that true celebration can be realized, rid of the carnal accessories of sensual practice, and free of the ritualized accouterments of religious tradition.

We believe in sanctification.

God's grace not only provides for our personal progress in purity and piety, but His Spirit flowing through our lives has a capacity to infuse our daily activities with righteousness. This means that amoral traditions may be seized upon by believers and converted to holy occasions and practices, so long as the Word and the way of the Lord are kept in primary focus. We resist as an inert, deadly religious, and nonscriptural notion the idea that participation in such festivals as Christmas and Easter are heathen practices to be shunned by believers. Instead, we hold that only believers have a concept which allows for the fullest and richest celebration at such times. We do not flee the innocent cultural traits of celebration, but choose to instill them with deeper color by participating with enlightened understanding and pure living.

We believe in symbolism.

No one can verify the calendar date of Jesus' birth, but we accept December 25 as an annual day of declaration that "The Word became flesh," and that "Light has come unto the world." No one can validate the giving of gifts as a divinely appointed means of celebration, but since we serve a gift-giving God (James 1:17), we believe it appropriate to signal the occasion of His Greatest Gift as a time of sharing in the same spirit of love. Although no one can make a "biblical case" for Christmas trees, we gather around ours with joy. We see in its living branches a symbol of everlasting life given us because of Jesus' death on *The Tree,* at Calvary—whose naked crossbars Xed out death and ushered in forgiveness, regeneration, and eternal hope.

. . . The lights on our tree gleam a testimony of His Light-of-the-world glory.

. . . The ornaments reflect the decorative splendor with which His kindnesses festoon our personal and corporate lives.

. . . The star beams hope, with a heavenward ray, reminding us that it is from there He shall come again to receive us.

The season is upon us, and in celebrating it we make it His! For He has made all of life's loveliest things ours.

Unto Jesus be

Winter Carol

Steel blue the sky and chill the night,
In which our Father gave the Light;
 Sent to warm our souls and
 to drive away the cold.
Let a carol rise, Noel, Noel, Noel;
Lift your voice, my soul, Noel, Noel.

Gray are the days of frosty clime,
Early the dusk at wintertime
 When we sing anew how
 the Morningstar appeared
Let a carol rise, Noel, Noel, Noel;
Dark no longer feared, Noel, Noel.

Short tho' our days and soon our night,
Flick'ring our flame and dim our light;
 Yet eternal life has been
 giv'n to man this Day.
Let a carol rise, Noel, Noel, Noel;
Sing now and for aye, Noel, Noel.

Snowfall and starlight everywhere,
Glory surrounds this season rare;
 For the Son of God now
 has come to us from heav'n.
Let a carol rise, Noel, Noel, Noel;
Grace and peace are giv'n, Noel, Noel.[19]

glory, honor, and

Praise Majesty,

NOTES

January

1. Jack Hayford, "In God's Own Time," © 1988 Maranatha! Music. All rights reserved. Used by permission. International copyright secured.

February

2. Edward Henry Joy, "All Your Anxiety" (London: Salvationist Publishing & Supplies, Ltd.).

3. Jack Hayford, "How Long the Night" (n.p.).

March

4. Jack Hayford, "Hear the Upward Call" (n.p.).

5. Jack Hayford, "All Is Well", © 1981, Rocksmith Music, c/o Trust Music Management Inc., P.O. Box 9256, Calabasas, Calif. 91372. Used by permission. All rights reserved.

April

6. Jack Hayford, "Build a Son, Lord" (n.p., 1962).

May

7. Jack Hayford, "Behold the Living God," © 1971, Canticle Publishing, Inc., Leawood, Kan. Used by permission.

June

8. Jack Hayford, "Great Deliverance—Mighty Redemption," ©1984, Maranatha! Music. All rights reserved. Used by permission. International copyright secured.

July

9. Jack Hayford, "Thou, God, Seest Me" (n.p., 1977).

August

10. Jack Hayford, "Triumphal Reentry" (n.p., rev. 1990).

September

11. Jack Hayford, "Teach Me about Thy Cross," © 1987, Maranatha! Music. All rights reserved. Used by permission. International copyright secured.

October

12. Jack Hayford, "I've Never Taken It Away" (n.p., 25 June 1989).

November

13. Henry Alford, "Come, Ye Thankful People."

14. Ibid.

15. Jack Hayford, "All This Slendor," ©1983 Maranatha! Music. All rights reserved. Used by permission. International copyright secured.

16. Jack Hayford, "A Gift of Thanksgiving," ©1986, Maranatha! Music. All rights reserved. Used by permission. International copyright secured.

December

17. Jack Hayford, "On This Christmas Day," ©1987, Maranatha! Music. All rights reserved. Used by permission. International copyright secured.

18. Jack Hayford, "The Light Has Come," ©1980, Maranatha! Music. All rights reserved. Used by permission. International copyright secured.

19. Jack Hayford, "Winter Carol," © 1988 Maranatha! Music.   All rights reserved. Used by permission. International copyright secured.

APPENDIX

The following songs and choruses were authored and arranged by Jack Hayford. Excerpts from the lyrics appear in calligraphy on the page indicated.

Page 22

Lord, You cause my heart to laugh and make my mouth to
   sing.
Lord, You fill my lips with praise and now the praises ring
For the joy of Your way increases ev'ry day
And I find my hands are reaching out in love.

So I'm reaching up, expressing love and thanks to Thee,
And I'm reaching out to join the hands of those by me.
For the joy of your way increases ev'ry day
And I find my hands are reaching out in love.

Page 40

It's me, Lord,
Just me, Lord;
I long to be free, Lord,
So I come to Thee, Lord,
   with my heart in my hands.

I pray, Lord,
Today, Lord,
That You'll have Your way, Lord;
It's me, Lord,
Just me, Lord,
Set me free.

274

Nobody Cared, ©1969, Pilot Point Music, Kansas City, Mo.
Used by permission.

Nobody wanted Him; nobody cared.
Nobody wanted Him; no one shared
in the promise He brought as a babe that night.
Nobody, nobody, nobody cared.

Nobody lauded Him; nobody sang.
No crowd applauded Him; no bells rang
When He went to the desert to fast and pray.
Nobody, nobody, nobody cared.

But, oh, how the thousands came when the bread was
      multiplied!
And, oh, how the hosannas rang at their King's triumphant
      ride!
And as long as the miracles flowed like wine,
They called Him Wonderful,
They came to dine.

Nobody wanted Him; no one remained.
They only taunted Him when His Cross was stained
With the blood freely given for a world enchained.
Nobody, nobody, no one but nobody came.

I've Got the Life of God in Me, ©1987, Maranatha! Music,
All rights reserved. Used by permission. International
copyright secured

All around in the ground there's a message,
A simple truth that can set you free.
It's alive in every seed,
and it can free you indeed.
When the truth you begin to see.

The God who made all creation around you,
With just a word made all the world
and all it holds;
Has placed within every flower
All of His mighty power
And each blossom has a message to unfold.

Chorus:

I've got the life of God in me,
I've got the life of God in me,
The power that made all the universe
with just a word
Has come to live in me
abundantly.
Just like a seed becomes a tree,
Just like a stream becomes the sea,
I believe I'll receive what God has promised me,
For His Word is at work within me mightily,

What He's begun, like the sun, will rise triumphantly,
Because the life of God's in me,
I've got the life of God in me.

Page 104   **Holy Spirit, Come,** ©1988, Maranatha! Music.
All rights reserved. Used by permission. International
copyright secured

Holy Spirit, come; let this be Your home;
Come and dwell among all of us who sing this song.
Come into this place; shine on ev'ry face;
Fill us with Your love and grace; Holy Spirit, come.

Page 124   **Come and Be King,** ©1981, Maranatha! Music.
All rights reserved. Used by permission. International
copyright secured

Come and be King, come even now,
Now as we sing, here as we bow,
Come and be King, Jesus be Lord,
Here as You're praised and adored.
See every heart open to You,
Uplifted hands now inviting
Jesus be King here in this place,
Come now and rule by Your grace.

Hear as we pray, "Your Kingdom come,"
Singing we say, "Your will be done."
Come and be King, conquering sin,
Jesus, we welcome You in.
Cleanse every heart with holy fire,
Let tongues of flame rest upon us.
Jesus be King here in this place,
Come now and rule by Your grace.

Glory to God, Father of love,
Praise to His Son, reigning above,
Spirit of truth, thanks be to Thee,
Worship we God, One in three.
Almighty One, O Holy Lord,
There is no god like unto Thee.
Jesus be King, here in this place,
Come now and rule by Your grace.

O how we yearn, come back again,
Jesus, return, Savior of men.
Tho' we rejoice now in Your power,
Longing we pray for that hour.
Trumpets will sound, clouds roll away,
Then every eye shall behold You.
Until that day, ever will sing,
Lord Jesus, come and be King.

276

Page 146   **There Is Nothing Impossible,** ©1974, Rocksmith Music,
c/o Trust Music Management, Inc., P.O. Box 9256,
Calabasas, Calif. 91372. Used by permission.

Join your hand with mine, let our faith combine
For in prayer there is nothing impossible.

For when two agree, pray in harmony,
Jesus said, "There is nothing impossible."

Let us come before the throne of God,
Let us call to Him in prayer
And in Jesus' name His promise claim,
Knowing He will answer our prayer.

Join your hand with mine, let our faith combine
For in prayer there is nothing impossible.

Come without a doubt, let your heart cry out
I believe there is nothing impossible.

Page 168   **Father God,** ©1973, Rocksmith Music,
c/o Trust Music Management, Inc., P.O. Box 9256,
Calabasas, Calif. 91372. Used by permission.

Father God,
I give all thanks
and praise to Thee

Father God,
My hands I humbly
raise to Thee

For Thy mighty pow'r
and love amazes me,

Amazes me, and I stand
in awe and worship
Father God.

Page 190   **Cleansing Power,** ©1976, Rocksmith Music,
c/o Trust Music Management, Inc., P.O. Box 9256,
Calabasas, Calif. 91372. Used by permission.

Cleansing power in this hour,
Wash my heart and all sin erase.
Blood of Jesus, flow and free us;
Lead us, Lord, to Thy resting place.

Page 210

Chosen, ©1985, Maranatha! Music.

Wond'ring and wand'ring I once lived my life
Wond'ring why? Who am I? Why was I made?
Wand'ring and searching for reasons to live
Then my eyes opened wide and Christ helped me see:
I am

Chosen to royalty, chosen for destiny,
Chosen by God's own hand.
Now I can stand
For since Jesus rules in me
I'm filled with His beauty;
Now it's my duty
To live like a chosen one.

Into my darkness He walked with His light,
Bringing day, healing rays restoring my sight.
Then Jesus Creator breathed into me
Identity, security, His love made me free.
Now I'm

Chosen to royalty, chosen for destiny,
Chosen by God's own hand.
Now I can stand
For since Jesus rules in me
I'm filled with His beauty;
Now it's my duty
To live like a chosen one.

Page 230

The Jesus of Revelation, ©1989, Maranatha! Music.

Glory and honor, praise and thanksgiving,
to Jesus the Lord of Lords, the Lamb who was slain.

Blessing and power, strength and all wisdom
be unto Him forevermore, the King of all Kings.

Once dead, now risen; living forever is Jesus,
the Lord of Lords, the Lamb who was slain.

Mighty in battle, leading to triumph,
He has the keys of death and hell and rules over all.

Lion of Judah, Alpha, Omega,
the First and Last, the Son of Man, the Faithful Amen.

Just as you promised, Jesus, come quickly
until you do we look for You, the Bright Morning Star.

278

Page 250
That You Came, ©1982, Maranatha! Music.

That You came is a wonder to me.
That You came in a manner so lowly,
Came to earth to live,
Came Your life to give.
That you came changed all history.

That You came brought the glorious Word,
Son of Man named "Jesus the Savior."
What a gift the Father gave;
His only Son He sent to save me.
That You came changed my destiny;
That You came is wonder to me.

Majesty, ©1981, Rocksmith Music,
c/o Trust Music Management, Inc., P.O. Box 9256,
Calabasas, Calif. 91372. Used by permission.

Majesty, worship His majesty.
Unto Jesus be all glory, honor, and praise.

Majesty, kingdom authority
flow from His throne unto His own;
His anthem raise.

So exalt, lift up on high the name of Jesus.
Magnify, come glorify Christ Jesus, the King.

Majesty, worship His majesty;
Jesus who died, now glorified, King of all kings
Jesus who died, now glorified, King of all kings
Worship His majesty.